18894
801.953

YORK NOTES

General Editors: Professor A.N. Jeffares (*University of Stirling*) & Professor Suheil Bushrui (*American University of Beirut*)

...on High Sc...
...orary Resource Centre

Tom Stoppard

PROFESSIONAL FOUL

Notes by Benedikte Uttenthal

MA (CAMBRIDGE) MA (ESSEX)
Education Officer,
H.M. Institution, Polmont

LONGMAN
YORK PRESS

LIBERTON HIGH SCHOOL

YORK PRESS
Immeuble Esseily, Place Riad Solh, Beirut.

LONGMAN GROUP UK LIMITED
Longman House, Burnt Mill, Harlow,
Essex CM20 2JE, England
Associated companies, branches and representatives
throughout the world

© Librairie du Liban 1984

All rights reserved; no part of this publication may be
reproduced, stored in a retrieval system, or transmitted
in any form or by any means, electronic, mechanical,
photocopying, recording, or otherwise, without
the prior written permission of the copyright owner.

First published 1984
Second impression 1990

ISBN 0-582-79266-5

Produced by Longman Group (FE) Ltd.
Printed in Hong Kong

Contents

Part 1

Introduction

The life and work of Tom Stoppard

The name Tom Stoppard, so plainly English, might lead us to think that *Professional Foul* was written by a native-born Englishman. This is far from the truth. By a series of dramatic twists of fate, Tom Stoppard, born and, initially, brought up in Czechoslovakia, became a British citizen. In studying *Professional Foul* we meet him when he was manifesting his interest in the country of his birth for the first time. This was after more than fifteen years as a playwright and thirty-one years of living in England. So far, it is his first and only play which is set in Czechoslovakia. But more interestingly, it is in many ways a summing up of subjects debated in his previous plays, most notably *Jumpers* (1972) and *Travesties* (1974; published 1975). Later we shall look more closely at the links between these two plays and *Professional Foul* and its setting.

Tom Stoppard was born in Zlin, Czechoslovakia, on 3 July 1937, the youngest son of Eugene Straussler and his wife Martha. His father was employed as a company doctor with the large Czechoslovak shoe company, Bata. Not long before the German invasion, Bata transferred much of their business out of Czechoslovakia and the Straussler family moved to Singapore. Here they were threatened with the Japanese invasion in 1942, and Martha and her two sons were evacuated to India. Eugene Straussler stayed behind and died in enemy hands. Tom Stoppard's most vivid—and, according to him, nostalgic—early childhood memories are of India. Mrs Straussler and the two boys were not left badly off. Stoppard eventually attended an American school in Darjeeling and his mother became the manageress of the Bata shoe shop there. To use Stoppard's own words, 'we were just living the ordinary sort of life of a working mother with two sons. But quite soon after the war my mother remarried—an Englishman in the British army in India, name of Stoppard'. His stepfather, Kenneth Stoppard, took his new family back to England in 1946 and pursued a career in the machine tool business. He sent his stepsons to preparatory and boarding grammar (that is, publicly financed) schools and Tom left school 'thoroughly bored by the idea of anything intellectual'. He did not consider a university education and joined the *Western Daily Press* in Bristol as an apprentice journalist straight from school in 1954. He proved to have a talent for writing and was quickly entrusted with writing features and occasional descriptive articles. This was at a time, 1956, when the British and French went into Suez and the Russians went into Budapest. Stoppard was beginning to take an interest in ontology* and ethics. However, 1956 was also notable for another event. It marked a significant change in the state of the British theatre.

The theatre in Britain had until then been in something of a rut. It was mainly supplying escapist, middlebrow entertainment, serious drama being provided by classical revivals and imports from America and Europe. George Bernard Shaw had died in 1950, Sean O'Casey was no longer writing plays, the talents of D.H. Lawrence, James Joyce, and T.S. Eliot lay more outside the theatre than in it. Writers who had made their name initially or principally through the theatre did so by writing light-weight melodrama and comedies (such as those of W. Somerset Maugham and Noël Coward). No doubt competition from the cinema and from the new medium of television, plus a lack of state subsidies, had helped to bring about the decline.

Then, in 1956, the English Stage Company was established under the direction of George Devine with a policy of promoting new drama of intellectual rigour. 'Ours is not to be a producer's theatre.' The new company started cautiously with two plays by novelists in their forties (Angus Wilson's (*b.* 1913) *The Mulberry Bush* and Arthur Miller's (*b.* 1915) *The Crucible*), and put on the unknown John Osborne's (*b.* 1929) *Look Back in Anger* as an act of faith. It was after all their policy to find new talent and to nurture it. Osborne was an obscure twenty-seven-year-old actor and this was his first play on the London stage. For all its faults this was the play that most successfully publicised the new style and subject matter which were awakening the interest of new writers in the theatre, and which were attracting an audience that was younger and came from a wider social spectrum than before. Indeed, its brash voice of protest, which still annoys some of its critics, made the awakening vigorous and memorable. The subject matter thought suitable for the London stage now included political protest and less affluent milieux. *Look Back in Anger* set a new tone of seriousness and provocation. Indeed much of the drama of this genre could well be accused of humourlessness and of political tub-thumping (as in the case of Arnold Wesker and John Arden), but for the first time audiences were invited to face social issues in realistic contemporary settings. The success of the English Stage Company seemed to rest on this one play, whereas in reality, a combination of fortunate decisions in casting and wise choices of plays, with new ventures being underwritten by popular classics, ensured its commercial survival. Television proved no

* This and other terms in Part 1 with which the reader may not be familiar are explained in the Notes and Glossary on pp.17–20.

longer a rival, but an ally. *Look Back in Anger* was in fact running at a loss until a brief extract was shown on television. Immediately the takings jumped to a comfortable margin of profit, and the author and the Royal Court found themselves famous. The fluent journalistic wit of Kenneth Tynan (1927–80) seized on the new opportunities offered by the theatre and helped to consolidate the public's interest through newspaper articles and script reading for theatres. In Stoppard's own words: 'After 1956 everybody of my age who wanted to write, wanted to write plays—after Osborne and the rest at the Court, and with Tynan on *The Observer*, and Peter Hall about to take over the RSC. In a sense I was writing plays for Tynan and Peter Hall.' (Peter Hall was one of the period's young star directors who by 1960 was in charge of the world-famous Royal Shakespeare Company (RSC) at Stratford-upon-Avon, having started his London career with notable productions of Samuel Beckett (*b.* 1906), Ugo Betti (1892–1954) and Jean Anouilh (*b.* 1910).) However, it was the sense of something happening and the encouragement of talent that moved Stoppard, rather than the political and social aspects of the change, for we shall see that for his first ten years there was little social commentary or politics in Stoppard's plays.

In 1958, Stoppard moved from the *Western Daily Press* to the *Bristol Evening News*, and in this new post he started wanting to write for the theatre. While on an Italian holiday in 1960, he suddenly decided to become a writer and on his return handed in his notice to the newspaper, retaining two weekly columns for his bread-and-butter. He finished his first play in about three months, working in a panic because 'I hadn't done any of the things by the age of twenty-three that I'd intended doing by the age of twenty-one; so I was doing everything two years late, and really had to get down to it'. That first play completed in 1960 was *A Walk on the Water* (see Part 5, Suggestions for further reading, p.72) which was revised for several productions, and finally published in 1968 as *Enter a Free Man*. As so many first works, it was unintentionally derivative; Stoppard has in retrospect nicknamed it 'Flowering Death of a Salesman' after the two plays that were its inspiration: Robert Bolt's (*b.* 1924) *Flowering Cherry* (1957) and Arthur Miller's (*b.* 1915) *Death of a Salesman* (1949). His next play, *The Gamblers* (unpublished but produced at Bristol University in 1965) was almost as derivative and again later earned a Stoppardian nickname: 'Waiting for Godot in the Condemned Cell'. However, he was building his reputation as a writer and making valuable contacts in the world of the theatre and its literary agents. He landed a job in London on *Scene* magazine, writing theatre reviews for almost a year, managed to publish a few short stories (see Part 5, Suggestions for further reading, p.74) and have a play (*M is for Moon Among Other Things*) performed on radio. Financially he was kept going by selling the options for *A Walk on the Water*. It was eventually twice shown on television (1963 and 1964) and finally in the theatre in 1968, revised as *Enter a Free Man*. This theatre production came two years after the production of his first real success in 1966 of *Rosencrantz and Guildenstern are Dead*.* By then *Enter a Free Man* seemed very much like old hat to Stoppard, who had developed a more independent style and way of thought in *Rosencrantz*.

He began writing *Rosencrantz* in 1964, on a Ford Foundation Scholarship which took him to Berlin on a colloquium for young playwrights. 'We were fed and housed in great comfort and just asked to get on with it. Of course, it was quite incapacitating.' Nevertheless *Rosencrantz* germinated in these conditions. It finally flowered as a hybrid of 'a play of ideas and farce or perhaps even high comedy'. It was the first of his plays to set the pattern for a blend of philosophy and comedy played against a background of political intrigue. *Jumpers, Travesties, Every Good Boy Deserves Favour* (1977; published 1978), *Professional Foul, Night and Day* (1978), *Dogg's Hamlet and Cahoot's Macbeth* (1979; published 1980) all follow this pattern, and when considered chronologically, each play takes some of the philosophical or moral arguments used in the previous play a few steps further. *Rosencrantz* was a playful, if tentative, beginning to Stoppard's epistemological and moral theatrical debates. Both Stoppard's method and the stage of his debate are illustrated by this comment he made about the play: 'There is very often *no* single, clear statement in my plays. What there is, is a series of conflicting statements made by conflicting characters ... an argument, a refutation, then a rebuttal of the refutation, then a counter-rebuttal, so there is never any point in this intellectual leap-frog at which I feel *that* is the speech to stop it on, that is the last word.' This leap-frog of ideas was to be typical of his writing until 1977, the year of *Professional Foul*, when it became clear to his audience that he had changed to a more committed stance.

Rosencrantz and Guildenstern are two marginal characters in Shakespeare's *Hamlet*. In Stoppard's play they are given the eerie property of appearing not to have an active existence outside the plot of *Hamlet* and no power to influence this plot. They are trapped by inexorable events whose purpose and direction are not clear. They pass their time in talking: 'We move idly towards eternity, without possibility of reprieve or hope of an explanation' says Guildenstern, who has much in common with Vladimir in Beckett's play *Waiting for Godot*, as Rosencrantz has much in common with Estragon. There can be no doubt that Beckett had inspired the play. Stoppard's two protagonists

---

* This play is henceforth referred to as *Rosencrantz*.

could ultimately be seen as being in a situation analogous to that of mankind. At any rate, the helplessness of Rosencrantz and Guildenstern reduces their needs to passing the time as entertainingly as possible. Stoppard's own need as playwright was, he said, 'to inject some sort of interest and colour into every line' to retain the audience's attention, rather than relying on the plot. Perhaps we should take this as a warning not to impute too much seriousness to the early works of Stoppard. However, we have a typically Stoppardian play of words and ideas in *Rosencrantz* even if in a largely borrowed setting. Here he uses comic devices that are also found in Beckett's *Godot*, such as direct appeals to the audience, puns, games, and aphorisms. He employs similar uncertainties of time, place, and memory, but is much more interested than Beckett in the jargon and speculations of various branches of philosophy—directly in probability and syllogisms, and more indirectly in free will, human identity and the moral nature of the universe. These were the interests on which he was to focus more sharply ten years later. The play is a still noticeably derivative picture of our human predicament, rendered with humour, sometimes with whimsy, and always with a compassionate pessimism. In the intellectual leap-frog, the questions, of course, remain unanswered. This is the early Stoppard at his most characteristic, writing being the way of 'arguing respectably with myself' and then perhaps 'of withdrawing with style from [the] chaos' of life. Later, in 1968, in an article for *The Sunday Times*, he wrote, 'I burn with no causes. I cannot say that I write with any social objectives. One writes because one loves writing, really'. It took some time for *Rosencrantz* to reach the stage. Eventually it was put on at the Fringe of the Edinburgh Festival in the summer of 1966 and from there, with the acclaim of *The Observer* critic Ronald Bryden, and the support of Kenneth Tynan, then literary manager of the National Theatre, it reached that theatre in London in the spring of 1967. It was a great success and earned Stoppard a good deal of money. The public revelled in its blend of the comic with intellectual games set in a frightening existential framework. It was very much a play of the nineteen-sixties, reflecting the style and preoccupations of that period. Stoppard was now famous.

Until these heady days, he had gone on doggedly with his career as an independent writer; three plays for radio had been produced (see Part 5, Suggestions for further reading); his first, and so far his only novel *Lord Malquist and Mr Moon* was published in 1965 (selling only four hundred and eighty-one copies in its first year); and his bread and butter had been earned at the BBC by writing the diary of an imaginary Arab student in London, which was then translated into Arabic and broadcast on the Overseas Service. Unfortunately the BBC has not kept any of these scripts or broadcasts. After his success at the National

Theatre with *Rosencrantz* he wrote a few short comedies, *The Real Inspector Hound* (1968), *After Magritte* (1970; published 1971), which were, in his words, 'an attempt to bring off a sort of comic coup in pure mechanistic terms'. They contain much parody and pastiche, both verbal and theatrical (for example, *Inspector Hound* belongs to the subgenre of the country-house detective thriller), two qualities much in· evidence in his later and more substantial comedies *Jumpers* and *Travesties*.

Around 1970 Stoppard was reading the British logical positivists with 'fascinated revulsion'. He told Kenneth Tynan that he was unable to accept their view that value judgments were meaningless because they could not be empirically verified. The revulsion had inspired him to write a play in support of moral philosophy and *Jumpers* was the extraordinary result. It took off from ideas in some of his previous plays: the plot was from an earlier television play *Another Moon Called Earth*, the human pyramid came from *Rosencrantz*, the mechanics of the farce from *The Real Inspector Hound* and some of the hilarious and improbable imagery from *After Magritte*. This self-plagiarism is typical of Stoppard, but the commitment to the refutation of a philosophical stance with political consequences was entirely new. The play is immensely complicated in plot and action, being truly visual theatre and relying greatly on visual puns and farcical situations. However, it continues Stoppard's delight in parody: of university dons, of philosophical language, politicians, crooners, of stock characters like the detective and the caretaker, and so on. But unlike his previous comedies, many of these devices actually serve to deepen the meaning of the arguments of the play. To give an example, the evil Vice-chancellor's team of acrobats, the 'jumpers', illustrates the futile mental contortions of the logical positivists.

The action of the play is centred round the confusingly named moral philosopher George Moore. (The real-life G.E. Moore (1873–1958) was a famous exponent of linguistic philosophy, that is, he was at the other end of the philosophical spectrum to the play's George.) Throughout the play George is attempting to write a lecture refuting positivism and proving the existence of God. The lecture, inevitably, is a witty parody of lecture mannerisms and donnish digressions. George opposes the rationalist arguments by employing a mixture of intuition, empirical evidence and deductive reasoning. The small private world of George and his beautiful and possibly errant wife, Dotty, is constantly invaded by intrusions from the outside world, the effect of these invasions being heightened by the presence of a huge television screen which shows what seems to be a virtual *coup d'état* by some totalitarians, misleadingly named 'Radical Liberals'. The Vice-chancellor (or Chancellor of Vice), Archie Jumper, is of that party and serves as

Stoppard's warning that the philosophy of moral pragmatism logically leads to totalitarianism. As in *Enter a Free Man* and *Rosencrantz* the cards are stacked against the humble and lovable protagonist. George is a brave but forlorn figure; the Rad-Libs rule; George even fails to intervene in the coda dream sequence when Archie murders one of his renegade henchmen. Ironically George has failed because of his tolerance and his respect for reason. In many ways this has been the problem of Stoppard himself: he has been distanced from the world by his craft, by his love for words and ideas. His love of parody rather than satire could be seen as a symptom of his being afraid to take himself seriously, and his lack of commitment could be the reason for his building up scenes through contradiction. The same arguments could be applied to all his elaborate jokes, both verbal and visual. They could be the elegant exasperation of a man feeling defeated by the seriousness of reality and the inadequacy of words to grapple with the problems that are created by ourselves and are intrinsic to existence. But in *Jumpers* a step has been made towards involvement with the world; the play offers an oblique answer to the problem it poses through the warning of Archie's corrupt and inhuman power and through the pathos of the isolated George.

Stoppard claims a penchant for what he calls 'theatre of audacity', meaning, perhaps, drama inspired by the theatre of the absurd in its forms, but, unlike absurdist plays, committed to exploring the human condition. It is certainly the first of Stoppard's more purposeful plays, and, typically, it uses a comic framework to explore serious questions. *Jumpers* is 'an attack by a principled writer upon a society whose standards seem to him increasingly pragmatic, expedient and amoral'.* And in Stoppard's own words, it is 'a theist play, written to combat the arrogant view that anyone who believes in God is some kind of a cripple, using God as a crutch. I wanted to suggest that atheists may be the cripples, lacking the strength to live with the idea of God'.†

The two protagonists in *Rosencrantz* ruminated on philosophy, and the Player, on the nature of art. *Jumpers* developed the philosophical arguments, and *Travesties*, as well as continuing to illustrate the perils of a materialistic view of the world, reintroduces the artistic question. In Stoppard's own words, *Travesties* ultimately asks 'whether an artist has to justify himself in political terms *at all*';† Stoppard has also stated in the same interview that art is important for two reasons—first, 'it provides the moral matrix, the moral sensibility from which we make our judgments about the world', that is, it is not, or should not be, a

---

* Benedict Nightingale, *An Introduction to Fifty Modern British Plays*, Pan Books, London, 1982, p.418.
† Tom Stoppard, 'Ambushes for the Audience: Towards a High Comedy of Ideas', interview in *Theatre Quarterly*, IV, 14, May–July 1974.

political tool, and, second, art is best at making general statements, at providing 'universal perception'.

This debate about art in *Travesties* is undertaken in startling circumstances. The play opens with Stoppardian panache (compare the opening of *Jumpers*, *After Magritte*, and other plays). The three protagonists are in a Zurich library speaking Dadaist nonsense, quoting esoteric prose. from *Ulysses**, and conversing in Russian—just about the first understandable sound uttered is the imperative 'Ssssh!' from the librarian. The protagonists who are to put forward the various propositions are three unconnected but famous figures who were all in Zurich during World War I: James Joyce (1882–1941), author of *Dubliners* (1914), *Ulysses* (1922) and *Finnegans Wake* (1939), Tristan Tzara (1896–1963), the exponent of Dadaism, and Valdimir Ilyich Lenin (1870–1924), the Russian revolutionary leader and head of the first Soviet government. In Stoppard's fantasy, they all meet and are remembered by the fourth protagonist, Henry Carr. In real life, Carr was a minor official at the British Consulate in Zurich and played Algernon in Oscar Wilde's (1854–1900) play *The Importance of Being Earnest* (1895) in a production for which Joyce was the business manager. The play takes place in the somewhat senile mind of Carr, who undoubtedly distorts Joyce and Tzara (but significantly not Lenin) with caricature memories and this constitutes one of the travesties. Nevertheless the messages are clear enough. Joyce represents the independence of the artist from political events—'As an artist, naturally I attach no importance to the swings and roundabouts of political history', and his work *Ulysses* will 'leave the world precisely as it finds it'. Lenin represents the pragmatic, materialistic view: 'today, literature must become party literature. . . . Literature must become part of the common cause of the proletariat, a cog in the Social Democratic mechanism . . . I dare say there will be hysterical intellectuals to raise a howl at this. . . . Such outcries would be nothing more than an expression of bourgeois-intellectual individualism'. Tristan Tzara is a kind of mediator in that as a Dadaist, he is drawn simultaneously to both sides, supporting revolution in art as well as in politics and yet seeing art as the means of transcending the mean realities of life. In Carr's confused memory, Joyce and Tzara become entangled with him in a witty pastiche of Wilde's comedy. Here lie further travesties: the distortions of historical events and literary styles. Yet Carr too is a mouthpiece for Stoppard's concerns: in Act

---

* *Ulysses*, a novel by James Joyce (1882–1941), was first published in 1922. The novel is about a day's events in Dublin at the turn of the century. The main characters roughly correspond to those of the *Odyssey*, an epic poem describing the adventures of Odysseus or (in Latin) Ulysses, by the great ancient Greek poet Homer (*born c.*1000BC). Joyce's novel is regarded as seminal, being highly original in style with its variety of literary techniques, and in its range of subject matter.

I he gives moral justification for war, defines the artist, and places him outside notions of class: 'Revolution in art is in no way connected with *class* revolution'. And in Act II he refutes Karl Marx (1818–83)* succinctly. Conveniently he is at his clearest at these moments. (In some ways his role resembles that of George Moore of *Jumpers*, muddled, lovable and on the right side.) Let it now be said that Stoppard is less concerned with consistency or development of character than with the development of ideas. He cannot be considered as a dramatist who explores relationships between individuals in any psychological depth. Lenin alone escapes the distorting prism of Carr's memory. In Act II he quotes himself at some length (his secretary humourlessly quotes his biography at even greater length), and the very precision of his self-quotations in this otherwise imprecise and humourous mixture of pastiche and puns, improbabilities and philosophy, brings a chill to the play, a chill that must reflect the author's horrified awareness of the historical course of Marxist-Leninism. It has been argued by most critics that this destroys the artistic unity of the play. It does, however, reflect Stoppard's growing belief in the overwhelming importance of certain events and ideas, an ironic stance when considered in relation to Joyce's utterances in the play, but nevertheless the inevitable paradox of defending freedom, for which artistry may have been partly sacrificed here. But it could be argued that no protagonist wins the debate verbally in the play; the debate may actually be won by the supporters of independent art through the way the play is constructed, as they are given greater scope in the comedy, greater artistic licence, and more humane character traits. Lenin is isolated by his speeches which clearly indicate the violence and mass murders that were to follow the revolution. 'I mean, in purely mundane, boring statistical terms, which sometimes can contain the essence of a situation, it is simply true that in the ten years after 1917 fifty times more people were done to death than in the *fifty years* before 1917'.† He is isolated from the engaging comings and goings of the other protagonists and from the basic tone of the play created by the cheerful parodies and jokes. The clear inference from this mixture of comedy and politics can only be that 'Revolutionary Artist' is a contradiction in terms.

At the time of the publication of *Travesties*, Stoppard was becoming more and more involved with the plight of political nonconformists in

---

* Marx was a German social theorist. He collaborated with Friedrich Engels (1820–95) in works on politics and economic history. He held revolutionary and communistic views. His major work, *Das Kapital* (vol. 1 1867, completed by Engels after Marx's death), puts forward his theory of political economy. It is a criticism of the capitalist system; the remedy, according to Marx, lies in total abolition of private property effected by a class war.

† Tom Stoppard, 'Ambushes for the Audience: Towards a High Comedy of Ideas', interview in *Theatre Quarterly*, IV, 14, May–July 1974.

the Soviet bloc. By 1976 he had addressed a rally in Trafalgar Square, London, sponsored by the Committee Against Psychiatric Abuse. In February 1977 he travelled to Moscow with a representative of Amnesty International and met several victimised so-called dissidents. Stoppard has described the customs procedures at Moscow as 'frightening'; and *Professional Foul* contains just such a scene. In June 1977 Stoppard visited his contemporary Vaclav Havel (*b*. 1936), a persecuted Czech playwright who has undergone the pressures Stoppard escaped as an emigré. This was Stoppard's first visit to the country of his birth. Havel had been silenced by Husak's regime (Husak was appointed Dubcek's successor by the Russians after their invasion of Czechoslovakia in 1968) and briefly imprisoned, but the authorities had difficulty in drumming up evidence for sedition that could bring him to court. Eventually he was prosecuted on a minor charge. But meanwhile the persecutions went on in several debilitating ways: eviction from home, difficulty in finding work and that only of the most menial kind, and so on.

All of these encounters with East European nonconformists, his involvement with Amnesty International and with the Committee Against Psychiatric Abuse, left their mark on Stoppard. 1977 saw the premiere of *Every Good Boy Deserves Favour* (published jointly with *Professional Foul*). At this point, the reader should refer to Stoppard's own introduction to that play published in the recommended edition. Briefly, he was inspired to write the play partly by the writings of Russian dissidents and by a meeting with Victor Fainberg* who had been pronounced insane and sentenced to imprisonment in Soviet mental hospitals for his protest against the invasion of Czechoslovakia. Partly he was inspired by André Previn (*b*. 1929), the composer and principal conductor of the London Symphony Orchestra, who wanted Stoppard to write something which needed a full-size orchestra on stage. In the play, *Every Good Boy Deserves Favour*, the orchestra is a metaphor for an orchestrated, that is, totalitarian, society and its presence on stage is justified by the delusions of a genuinely insane patient in the hospital. He happens to have the same name, Ivanov, as the political prisoner who is represented by a 'dissident' or discordant instrument in the orchestra, and when outside pressure for the release of the political prisoner becomes too great, this allows the authorities to release both Ivanovs as a result of a deliberate confusion. Ivanov, the insane, is released because he is obviously not a dissident, and Ivanov, the dissident, is released because he is obviously not insane. This is farcical, but part of the logic of totalitarian double-think. In the play

---

* Victor Fainberg is a former Russian dissident and art critic who spent five years in Soviet mental hospitals and prisons. He was allowed to emigrate in 1974 and now campaigns from London for human rights in Soviet Russia.

Stoppard makes little effort to manufacture jokes as in his previous works. The visual metaphor of the orchestra has its humorous moments, but otherwise the humour is of the black variety drawn from the ridiculous if dangerous nature of the contortions the totalitarians have to go through in order to justify their actions.

The play makes a bold experiment in its use of an orchestra on stage. It has a very clear political message which follows logically from the debates of *Jumpers* and *Travesties*. Stoppard's growing personal involvement with the victims of the excesses of East European totalitarian regimes ensured that his plea for individual freedom was made more clearly than ever before.

His next play, *Professional Foul*, is closely related in topic as well as in its more serious presentation. It was written to mark Amnesty International's 'Prisoner of Conscience Year' (1977) and is dedicated to the Czech playwright Vaclav Havel, to whose work and personality Stoppard feels strongly drawn. 1977 was also the year of the Czech human rights protesters, the Chartists, who presented their government with a formal protest against its violations of the Helsinki human rights agreement. The fact that the play was written for television undoubtedly shows that Stoppard wished to carry out his debates about moral action in the face of totalitarianism in front of as large an audience as possible. The play is much simpler in structure than any of his previous works and is perhaps his most accessible. He is no longer the playwright who 'burns with no causes'.

1978 saw the production and publication of Stoppard's next stage play, *Night and Day*. Set in another kind of ruthless totalitarian regime, the fictitious black African state Kambawe, it is primarily concerned with the freedom of the press and secondarily with the action of trade unions. It is akin to *Professional Foul* in that it remains on the whole realistic, and it advances Stoppard's arguments to include African dictatorships and trade union closed shops in his criticisms. What there is of humour lies mainly in the joy of parody (press jargon, telex gobbledegook) and in the unexpected confrontation between the wife and her lover in front of her unsuspecting husband.

Dogg's Hamlet and *Cahoot's Macbeth* were performed and published in 1979, the former a comedy based on a dubious Wittgensteinian* proposition and the latter (linked to the former by one character and a coda of the Wittgensteinian word-game) a tribute to the dissident

---

* Ludwig Wittgenstein (1889–1951). The play, *Dogg's Hamlet*, is based on Wittgenstein's idea that one person's understanding of language need not coincide with another's, and in theory it would be possible in very special and limited circumstances for two people to carry out a task quite correctly while having completely different interpretations of each other's words. The necessary limitations of the circumstances make the proposition seem less than revealing. In *Dogg's Hamlet* Stoppard has tried to create such a language for the special circumstances of building a stage. The result is a funny, though not edifying, play.

Czech playwright Pavel Kohout.* He, and a small company of banned actors, are trying to survive professionally by hiring themselves out to private citizens and performing shortened plays in their homes. *Cahoot's Macbeth* is just such a shortened play. Apart from the basic situation, overt political criticism is provided by the sinister interruptions by a police inspector. In both plays there are self-plagiarising strains of comedy—elaborately constructed jokes both visual and verbal similar to ones found in Stoppard's earlier works.

Recently, in 1981, breaking away from his moral and political concerns, Stoppard adapted Johann Nestroy's (1801–62)† farce *Einen Jux will er sich machen* as *On the Razzle*. His latest play *The Real Thing* (1982) perhaps marks another change in the maturer Stoppard. It is his first play to deal primarily with relationships within a troubled marriage, but still, the major cause of the trouble seems to be a political clash between husband and wife, the latter falling for the naive and cliché-ridden criticism of the institutions of Western democracy made by a lusty brute of a man who poses as a political victim. It could be that the mature Stoppard will be turning his attention towards the exploration of character and relationships. So far, however, he has moved from uncommitted seriousness tempered by farce to an open support, though still tempered with humour, of 'Western liberal democracy, favouring an intellectual elite and a progressive middle class based on a moral order derived from Christian absolutes'.**

A note on the text

The works of Tom Stoppard are published by Faber and Faber Limited, London, and the first Faber edition (1978) of *Professional Foul* has been used for this study. It is published together with *Every Good Boy Deserves Favour*, which the student should read as well. *Professional Foul* was first shown on BBC TV in September 1977.

Study aids

1. Part 1 of these Notes unavoidably includes difficult words which must be understood by the student of Stoppard. A simple glossary of such words is given below, in 'Notes and glossary', p.17, but many

* Kohout (*b*. 1928), a Czechoslovak writer and dramatist, is in frequent difficulties with the Czech authorities because of his civil rights activities.
† Nestroy, an Austrian dramatist and comic actor, wrote comedies, many of which are still part of the repertoire in Germany and Austria. His writing is distinguished by aggressive satire, though *Einen Jux will er sich machen* is purely farcical.
** Stoppard, in K. Tynan, *Show People*, Weidenfeld and Nicolson, London, 1980.

should be looked up in works offering more detailed explanations, such as Abrams's *Glossary* mentioned in Part 5, Suggestions for further reading, encyclopedias or literary companions, such as *The Oxford Companion to English Literature* or *The Concise Oxford Companion to the Theatre*. Needless to say, no student should ever read a text or a work of criticism without a good general dictionary.

2. You should make sure you have understood and can remember the main points made in Part 1 by answering these questions:

(*a*) Where and when was Stoppard born?

(*b*) Name three important events which occurred in 1956.

(*c*) Who wrote *Look Back in Anger*, and why was it important?

(*d*) When did Stoppard start writing plays, and what was his first work?

(*e*) What was Stoppard's first success on the stage, and what characterises this play?

(*f*) What is *Jumpers* (1972) about?

(*g*) What is *Travesties* (1974) about? Who are the four protagonists?

(*h*) What do *Jumpers* and *Travesties* have in common with *Rosencrantz and Guildenstern are Dead*?

(*i*) What do *Jumpers* and *Travesties* have in common with *Professional Foul*?

(*j*) In what ways have Stoppard's concerns changed since the writing of *Rosencrantz* and in what ways is *Professional Foul* a manifestation of that change?

(*k*) Name two human rights movements in which Stoppard has been involved.

(*l*) What was the inspiration of *Every Good Boy Deserves Favour*?

(*m*) What was 1977 notable for?

NOTES AND GLOSSARY:
The words are given in the order in which they appear in the text above.

ontology: branch of metaphysics which studies the nature of existence

melodrama: a dramatic form in which exaggeration of effect and emotion is produced and plot or action is emphasised at the expense of characterisation:

epistemological: belonging to a branch of philosophy that investigates the origin, nature, and limits of human knowledge

protagonist: the leading character or hero of a drama or other literary work

syllogism: in logic, an argument expressed in the form of two propositions called the premises which lead to the conclusion, for example, 'All A is B; all B is C; therefore all A is C'

existential: pertaining to existentialism, which is a modern movement encompassing a variety of themes, among them the doctrine that man has absolute freedom of choice but that there are no rational criteria serving as a basis for choice, and that in general the universe is absurd. There is also an emphasis on the phenomena of anxiety and alienation

pastiche: a literary, musical, or artistic piece consisting of motifs or techniques borrowed from another source or sources

logical positivists: those belonging to a philosophical movement that arose in the 1920s influenced amongst others by Wittgenstein. It insisted that philosophy should be scientific, regarding it as an analytical rather than a speculative activity. They considered that any assertion has meaning only if it can be empirically tested. Metaphysical propositions and those of aesthetics and religion are consequently meaningless, since it is impossible to say how they can be verified

farce: a light, humorous play in which the plot depends upon a skilfully exploited situation rather than upon the development of character

pun: a play on words usually for humorous effect which relies on words which sound the same but have widely different meanings. The best puns use both such meanings appropriately, for example, 'Crisp's . . . comment . . . looked salt and vinegar flavoured' (*Professional Foul*, Scene 7)

donnish: pertaining to a don who is a head, fellow, or tutor of a college, usually in the universities of Oxford or Cambridge

empirical: derived from or verified by experience or experiment

totalitarianism: absolute control by a centralised government that grants neither recognition nor tolerance to parties of differing opinion

coda: normally a musical term meaning a more or less independent passage concluding a composition

renegade: a person who deserts a cause or party in favour of another

henchman: an unscrupulous supporter or adherent of a political figure or cause, especially one motivated by the hope of personal gain

theatre of the absurd: name given to plays that show that life is essentially without meaning or purpose and that human beings cannot communicate. This leads to the abandonment of dramatic forms and coherent dialogue, the futility of existence being conveyed by illogical and meaningless speeches and ultimately by complete silence. One of the first and perhaps most characteristic plays of this style was Beckett's *Waiting for Godot* (1952). This movement has made a profound impression on many other modes of drama

pragmatic: pertaining to a philosophical movement stressing practical consequences as constituting the essential criteria in determining truth, meaning, or value

materialistic: placing an emphasis on material objects and considerations, with a disinterest in or rejection of spiritual values

Dadaist: belonging to a group of artists and writers of the early twentieth century who exploited accidental and incongruous effects in their work and challenged established ideas of art, morality, and so on

ironic: irony is usually a figure of speech in which words express a meaning that is often the direct opposite of the intended meaning. In works of literature, irony can be indicated by the development of character or plot which results in attitudes or actions opposite to those actually or ostensibly stated. In works of drama, the irony is often perceived by the audience before the stage characters have grapsed the situation. In *Professional Foul* the central irony must be the crushing of individual freedom in a state where the constitution guarantees it. Other ironies are mostly centred on the character of McKendrick: a near-Marxist who writes for pornographic magazines; the inspirer of Anderson's good deed but also the victim of it, and so on

metaphor: a frequently used device for colouring language and enhancing its meaning by associating a person, object or situation with another object or situation it does not literally denote. For example, 'McKendrick is a rougher sort of diamond', or, 'A mighty fortress is our God'. Metaphors can be extended, though when this is done thoroughly the device is normally known as allegory, for example, the 'journey' of life in the medieval play *Everyman*. There is no doubt that the football match is used metaphorically in *Professional Foul*; it is not there for its literal occurrence only or for its mere convenience to the action of the play; it clarifies, for the viewer, the situation Anderson finds himself in so that he is *felt* to be a player in a philosophical game and one who manages to win a point by breaking a small rule—'felt' because metaphors often work well without reader's or viewer's being fully conscious of them; they work as an emotional device in art and can be particularly effective in making a reader or viewer appreciate a complex situation which would otherwise be beyond his immediate grasp. The philosophical background to the progression of Anderson's thinking is a case in point

Wittgensteinian: following the theories of Ludwig Wittgenstein (1889–1951), an Austrian philosopher, whose abiding preoccupation was with language, which he saw predominantly as a social phenomenon. He was a fundamental influence on the logical positivists

Part 2

Summaries
of PROFESSIONAL FOUL

A general summary

The play has sixteen scenes and ten different settings, the television camera and studio allowing for greater flexibility than the stage. We should, of course, never lose sight of the fact that unlike the plays discussed so far in Part 1, *Professional Foul* is written for television, and this makes it different from them in several respects.

We first meet Professor Anderson, a Cambridge don, aboard an aeroplane *en route* to Prague, ostensibly to attend a philosophical colloquium. A colleague, hitherto unknown to him, introduces himself to Anderson. It is McKendrick, also from a university, but a redbrick* one. Their conversation establishes to the audience that there is a connection, if only by implication, between the study of philosophy and politics, and that the political situation in Prague is not what it should be from their point of view.

Later, in the hotel lobby in Prague, Anderson is introduced to Chetwyn, the third philosopher from England, who was also on the plane. Anderson picks up an envelope from the reception desk and in the lift spots Broadbent and Crisp who we later realise are two footballers. When Anderson points them out to McKendrick, the latter mistakes them for philosophers.

Anderson goes to his hotel room where a former Czech student of his, Hollar, calls on him. He asks Anderson to smuggle out his thesis, which is about the ethics of the individual being the basis for ethics of the state. He wishes it to be published in England. He makes it clear that he is being watched by state agents because he is regarded as a dissident, and that he is likely to be imprisoned and have his thesis confiscated. Anderson refuses to smuggle out the thesis on the grounds that it would be a breach of good manners and a breach of his contract with the Czech state. But he does consent to look after it as Hollar fears it will be taken from him on the way home. Anderson agrees to take it to Hollar's flat the next day.

The next day in the morning, Anderson meets Crisp and Broadbent at the hotel lift and it is established that they are footballers and that

---

* A term used to describe English universities in the provinces, other than Oxford and Cambridge, both of which are largely built from limestone.

LIBERTON HIGH SCHOOL

Anderson's ulterior motive for coming to Prague is to see a football match. Anderson shows by his detailed knowledge of the game that he is a very keen football fan indeed, and his advice to the players later proves to be well founded. On the way down in the lift McKendrick again meets the two footballers and mistakes them for philosophers.

In the next scene (5) we are at the philosophical colloquium. McKendrick's mistake over the identity of the footballers is cleared up while he converses with Anderson during a linguistic philosopher's lecture on ambiguity. He also realises that Anderson will be attending the World Cup qualifying football match between Czechoslovakia and England in the afternoon. By both visual and verbal means, the limitations of linguistic philosophy are indicated.

Anderson departs early from the colloquium to take Hollar's thesis to his flat. The scene at the flat is one of confusion. Czech police are searching it and the distraught Mrs Hollar asks Anderson to be her witness during the search. Anderson does not wish to stay as he knows he is late for the football match, but is prevented from leaving by the police. He hears a snatch of the football match which is crucial to the dénouement on the radio. Broadbent has committed a professional foul. Shortly afterwards the police claim that they have found illegally hoarded foreign currency under the floorboards, the offence for which Hollar has already been arrested. It is obvious that the charge and the evidence have been manufactured by the police for political reasons. The foul of the match is contrasted with the foul action of the police. Hollar's son Sacha appears in the scene to comfort his mother.

Worn out, Anderson returns to his hotel. In the rooms next to his, he hears two English journalists dictating descriptions of the match over the telephone. He invites himself in to listen to their accounts.

In the evening Anderson dines in the hotel with his philosopher colleagues from the colloquium. During the trivial conversation, McKendrick reveals that his understanding of morality regarding the rights of individuals is profounder than Anderson's; unwittingly he provides a philosophical criticism of Anderson's decision about Hollar's thesis. We also learn that Chetwyn, like Anderson, had an ulterior motive for coming to the colloquium, though we do not learn exactly what it was. Mrs Hollar has been lingering in the hotel vestibule meanwhile, and when McKendrick draws Anderson's attention to her, Anderson leaves to talk to her through her son Sacha.

In the street, Sacha explains that his father has been arrested and that their home has been searched for twenty hours. When he is assured that Anderson still has his father's thesis, he begs him to hand it over to a friend of theirs, Jan, who will be at the colloquium the next day. Anderson is much troubled by their plight and assures them he will do all he can to help.

In the night Anderson ponders the situation and decides to borrow the typewriter of his neighbour Grayson, the journalist. McKendrick is in Grayson's room, drunk, together with the footballers Broadbent and Crisp. He is criticising them for the foul committed at the match. He sets out an argument against opportunism and once again reveals the underlying philosophical argument of the play. The footballer Broadbent (who committed the foul), finding his criticisms insulting, finally knocks McKendrick down. Anderson kindly steps in and helps McKendrick back to his room, saying that he will return for the typewriter.

At the colloquium the next day, Anderson delivers his lecture, but not the one submitted in advance to the colloquium. Instead he delivers a paper on the conflicts between the rights of individuals and the rights of the community, that is, a paper giving philosophical support to the basic human rights which have been flouted in Czechoslovakia, particularly, as far as Anderson is concerned, in the case of Hollar. It is also, of course, the same topic as Hollar's thesis. The Chairman of the colloquium attempts to stop Anderson, but when he fails, he consults his superiors and then organises a false fire alarm. Anderson has to stop his lecture and all the philosophers leave the hall. Meanwhile the camera has cut to McKendrick's room, where we see him suffering from a hangover amongst his half-packed luggage. It then cuts to Anderson's room where we see two policemen meticulously searching the room and his belongings.

At the airport we see the customs men and plain-clothes policemen searching the philosophers' luggage. Anderson is searched very thoroughly, but they find nothing. What has happened to Hollar's thesis? Chetwyn is also searched thoroughly, and the police find letters to Amnesty International and other bodies. Chetwyn is detained. McKendrick gets no more than a perfunctory search.

The play ends, as it started, in the aeroplane. McKendrick and Anderson discuss Chetwyn's fate, and Anderson lets McKendrick know that he too had something to hide. McKendrick asks where, and Anderson reveals that the previous night he placed Hollar's thesis in McKendrick's briefcase. He refers to one of McKendrick's philosophical arguments to justify his action when McKendrick becomes angry at his deception or 'professional foul'. Nevertheless, the thesis is now bound for the West.

Detailed summaries

STUDY HINT:
The following summaries of each scene will be of little use to you unless you have already read the play. You will need to refer to the text as you go along. If you do this carefully, you will pick up the habit of detailed

or analytical reading so that you will be able to understand and enjoy more of what you read, and also gain better marks in examinations.

Scene 1

It is Friday lunchtime. Unlike most of Stoppard's previous stage works, we are in a realistic as well as contemporary (1977) setting, in fact, in the cabin of a passenger jet. The camera focuses on two characters, Anderson (we never learn his Christian name) and Bill McKendrick. While both are the protagonists, the action centres round Anderson whom we follow in every scene.

Anderson is a middle-aged Cambridge Professor of Ethics (moral philosophy). He is fastidious, that is, careful and critical, while McKendrick, from a less prestigious university ('Stoke', as we learn moments later) is younger, about forty, and is a much less cautious character. It would be fair to say that Stoppard has with economy of detail presented us with recognisable British university types. We are almost immediately introduced to a significant stage property, a mildly pornographic magazine such as can commonly be bought at airports. Anderson begins to look at it under the cover of a glossy brochure which gives the television audience the purpose and destination of the flight by its title. It also allows them to see that both Anderson and McKendrick are heading for the same colloquium, as McKendrick too has the brochure. McKendrick catches sight of Anderson's brochure and seizes the opportunity to introduce himself. Anderson turns the conversation into a linguistic speculation: 'Young therefore old. Old therefore young,' and we are thereby at the very beginning introduced to the idea of ambiguity, the inadequacy of language, and of the need to search for truth. In the ensuing conversation, we learn more about the philosophical leanings of them both, and also of Chetwyn, the third English philosopher on the plane, who is asleep. Anderson states that he has an ulterior motive for coming to Czechoslovakia, but refuses to make McKendrick a co-conspirator.

Consequently neither he nor the television audience knows yet what that motive is, though our curiosity is aroused. We also learn something of the varying status of British universities, and of Anderson's fame and enviable position. But McKendrick is not humiliated for long, for he espies the sex magazine on Anderson's lap when the hostess removes his lunch tray and crudely believes he has found Anderson's weakness. There is a lot of humour in this opening scene: in the contrast and clashes of characters, in Anderson's detachment—partly a defence mechanism, partly a sympton of his status, in McKendrick's rashness, and in the cross-purposes of much of their conversation.

STUDY HINT:
Stoppard writes with such seemingly effortless naturalism that it is easy to fall into the trap of thinking that most of his lines contain little or nothing worthy of analysis. To think this would be a fatal mistake. There is hardly a line that does not contain a meaning or a purpose other than its immediate sense. Take one almost randomly picked line: 'Have you noticed the way the wings keep wagging?' It is (a) a realistic observation of aeroplane wings in flight, but more significantly, (b) a fact worrying Anderson—enough for him to mention it again later on in the scene, (c) it leads the reader to think that not only is Anderson fastidious, as the playwright says at the beginning of the scene, but anxious as well. He is not confident in all respects. The title of his philosophal paper for the colloquium, 'Ethical Fictions as Ethical Foundations' is a reflection of his own moral attitude at this stage. Anderson is not unlike George Riley, Rosencrantz and Guildenstern, and possibly George Moore—the Stoppardian heroes who, desiring to create for themselves some kind of order in a chaotic world, construct fictitious systems in which they can function. But to maintain these fictions, the characters often have to ignore the sufferings of other individuals. Rosencrantz and Guildenstern have relieved themselves of the responsibility of making moral choices in accepting the metaphor of life as a stage. George Moore in *Jumpers* has so retreated into theorising about morality that he is unable to act in the political arena where so much moral havoc is wreaked by the Rad-Libs. And Anderson, in constructing a moral framework of contracts and good manners, is at first unable to help his former student Hollar. Anderson is the clever but anxious Stoppardian hero in flight from the brutal realities of life, avoiding any action which disturbs his retreat from the fragility, complexity and menace of modern life, symbolised by the wagging aeroplane wings.

You should now ask yourself what McKendrick's line, 'I wonder if there'll be any decent women' tells us about him, and how it links with the development of the play.

NOTES AND GLOSSARY:

Oxbridge: a composite word from 'Oxford' and 'Cambridge', meaning either or both of the two élite British universities

fastidious: very careful and very critical

rougher sort of diamond: a metaphor, now really a cliché for an unrefined (unpolished) character, who nevertheless is fundamentally worth a lot

congress: a meeting of representatives of a party or a common interest, here of course, philosophers

Colloquium Philosophicum: philosophical group discussion

Prague 77: Prague is the capital of Czechoslovakia. 1977 was the year of the 'Charter 77' group when a formal protest (the Charter) was presented to the Czech government about their violation of the Helsinki agreements on human rights in 1975. Over three hundred leading Czech writers and intellectuals signed the Charter. The dedicatee of the play, Vaclav Havel, was one of the signatories and one of the three designated spokesmen. He was imprisoned in January 1977 by the Czech authorities

liquorice allsorts: an inexpensive mixture of soft sweets some of which are layered, some centred and some coated with liquorice

bunfights: schoolboy imagery of an enjoyable and sometimes boisterous meeting of like-minded people

faculty almoner: a university is usually divided into areas of study called faculties; for example Faculty of Philosophy. The almoner is a term sometimes used for the administrator, a non-academic functionary who looks after the money allocated to the faculty

Aristotle: (384−322BC) Greek philosopher chiefly known for his division of learning into what we now acknowledge as traditional subject areas, for example, logic, ethics, politics, metaphysics, biology, physics, psychology, poetry, rhetoric, and so on. He is also known as a critic of Plato (see Notes and Glossary, p.42) and his theory of a full reality outside this world, and of his dialectical method. Aristotle stressed the need for the active pursuit of moral and intellectual excellence. For Plato, knowledge itself was virtue

St Augustine: St Augustine of Hippo (354−430), the greatest of the early churchmen, the Latin fathers, author of the *Confessions* and *The City of God*. His philosophy is really subordinated to religious interests, but he saw both as quests for wisdom, and through wisdom, God's grace. Chetwyn is therefore well away from the main stream of British philosophy which is still centred on logical positivism, that is, close and elaborate consideration of language, accepting no statement that is not empirically verifiable so that no value judgement is considered truly meaningful

The Times:	the leading British newspaper in that it is considered the most serious, and by some the most objective
Ethically:	pertaining to ethics which is in this case a branch of philosophy dealing with values relating to human conduct, with the rightness or wrongness of certain actions, the goodness of otherwise of one's motives and purposes of such actions. Note that Anderson is Professor of Ethics (Scene 6)
Stoke:	an industrial city in England in the North Midlands, not known for its beauty
tits and bums:	vulgar expression for female breasts and buttocks
Marxists:	followers of the materialist philosopher Karl Marx (1818–83). By a series of extraordinary historical events not fitting his theories, his philosophy became the inspiration of the Soviet state
prudes:	people who are excessively proper or modest in conduct, speech and dress

I sail pretty close to the wind: that is, he runs the risk of transgressing Marxist codes or he is not completely Marxist in his views

travel broadens the mind: an English proverb

Scene 2

We are now in the lobby of a hotel in Prague on Friday afternoon. The camera makes sure we notice a young man who is watching the Englishmen. The television audience will not know for certain who he is as yet, though his dress and demeanour may allow plausible guesses. Anderson uses his standard response when he is introduced to Chetwyn (compare his response to McKendrick's university), which is meant to put the other man at his ease and is probably intended as an encouragement but nevertheless manages to be patronising. The clerk hands Anderson an envelope. Again the television audience do not yet know what it contains. Anderson spots Crisp and Broadbent, who once more are stock types, fit and uneducated-looking ('flashy suit'). Typically, McKendrick with Marxist-style wishful thinking mistakes them for up-and-coming philosophers (there is some irony in this situation), though it is probably obvious to the audience that this is highly unlikely, as it is also probably obvious that Anderson's comments about them concern football, whereas McKendrick mistakes them for political attitudes within the study of philosophy. This misunderstanding is based on punning, for example, the two meanings of left-wing, and is a typical Stoppardian device. Chetwyn's automatic response in calling Anderson

'Sir' reflects, apart from their age-gap, Anderson's own style of address to him earlier on. We might conclude that Anderson has brought it on himself, and his discomfort is mildly humorous, as is Chetwyn's eagerness to flatter.

NOTES AND GLOSSARY:

Birmingham: a large industrial city in the centre of England, not noted for its beauty

Only of philosophy: a self-deprecatory remark, showing McKendrick's excessive class-consciousness. Again this is not without irony considering his self-confessed political leanings. His idea is that doctors of medicine somehow have a higher social status than people who have gained doctorates by written dissertations in other subjects

opportunist: this will be seen to have a philosophical meaning later in the play (see McKendrick's drunken accusation in Scene 10)

tragic heroes: Aristotle's short treatise on drama, particularly tragedy, is called the *Poetics*. In it he discusses structures and events that are proper to real tragedy, one being the fall of the truly great, for example, the undoing of a king as in *Oedipus Rex*

Scene 3

We move on chronologically. It is later on the same day, and we are now in Anderson's hotel room, which has an adjoining bathroom. Once again our attention is drawn to the pornographic magazine, so it becomes obvious that it has some dramatic significance apart from being a mild joke on at least three levels: Anderson is embarrassed by it and his rigid attitude seems mildly funny; the danger of having it in a Marxist totalitarian country seems out of all proportion to its contents; and there is the willingness of the semi-Marxist McKendrick to write for such magazines which seems out of place considering his training *and* his political leanings. When there is a knock on the door, Anderson tosses it into his suitcase, and opens the door to Pavel Hollar whom he does not recognise at first. Every time Anderson has met anybody so far, we see that instinctively he is adept at distancing himself, being little concerned with other people and their circumstances. When he eventually recognises Hollar, his joviality is forced; he has forgotten that Hollar was a first-class student of his and cannot at first get his brain to accommodate the idea of his being a cleaner. This is not only a symptom of his remoteness from reality, but also a comment on the degree of wasteful cruelty with which the Czech regime treats its independently-minded intellectuals. This scene is of dramatic significance in the play: it marks Anderson's confrontation with an unacceptable reality and it also marks his first response to it, withdrawal based on an 'ethical fiction', the fiction that good manners and the rules of contracts prevent his taking Hollar's dissident thesis out of Czechoslovakia. The irony is that Hollar's thesis is actually about correct behaviour, and argues against Anderson's way of thinking. However, Anderson is clever enough to see a flaw in his own argument about contractual obligations, that is, in both his and Hollar's case it cannot be argued that all terms in the Czech state's contract have been entered into freely. But Hollar goes further: individuals simply have inherent rights and they are paramount. This is so clear that even a child, his son, can see it. (So too can Chetwyn's son in Scene 8). But Anderson loses patience at that point and starts to move away, back to his room. Hollar follows him.

Anderson cannot at first believe that his room may be bugged, but Hollar's elaborate anti-bugging tactics (the eraser pad, leaving the room, running the bath) build up an atmosphere of tension intensified by Anderson's bewilderment. We learn of Hollar's harassment by the authorities; he expects to be imprisoned; he is under close scrutiny; and his contacts and friendships are limited and monitored (his telephone has been removed). Even Anderson's neighbour, who appears while they speak in the corridor, seems sinister—is he a state agent? we are made to ask. But his shapeless suit is not the attire of a Czech plainclothes policeman. He is an English journalist, Grayson, as we learn later in Scene 7, a joke that is better appreciated on the printed page than on the television screen. There is too, a little ironic humour in Hollar's closing remark 'Welcome to Prague' which turns to fear as we listen with Anderson to the ominous approaching footsteps.

NOTES AND GLOSSARY:

Thomas Paine: (1737−1807), an English writer and political theorist, who published in 1791−2 *Rights of Man* in reply to Edmund Burke's (1729−97) *Reflections on the Revolution in France* (1790). While Burke believed that the common good was best secured by responsible aristocratic govenment, Paine defended democracy and republican principles

Locke: John Locke (1632−1704), a British philosopher whose two *Treatises of Government* (1690) were greatly influential in forming modern concepts of liberal democracy

bugged: having a hidden microphone so that conversations can be secretly overheard

Reading:	the University of Reading. Reading is a city in southern England
Leicester:	the University of Leicester. Leicester is a city in central England known chiefly for its textile and footwear industries
calumny:	a false and malicious statement designed to injure someone's or something's reputation; slander; defamation. Not the best word to use here. 'Iniquity' would have been more appropriate
writ big:	idiomatic mistake by Hollar, corrected by Anderson
Mr Husak:	Gustav Husak (*b.* 1913). In April 1969 after the deposition of Dubcek by the Russians, he became first secretary of the Czech Communist Party, and so leader of its regime. He is now the President of Czechoslovakia.

Scene 4

It is now Saturday morning in Anderson's room on the ninth floor, the first day of the colloquium, as we are reminded by the camera resting on its brochure. We follow Anderson to the lift, which is slow to arrive. This little detail indicates a playwright who has travelled in the Soviet bloc, but more to the point of the play, it is yet another sticky thread in the web of discomfort which enmeshes the individual in a totalitarian state. If the individual is subordinated to the state, it follows both logically and in practice that the finer details of his needs and comforts are disregarded. At the lift Anderson encounters one of the footballers, Crisp, and introduces himself to him. Broadbent arrives and Anderson shows him, unnecessarily, and us, with more purpose, that the envelope collected from the hotel reception contains his ticket for the football match. They enter the lift and descend towards the lobby. Anderson reveals that he is a very knowledgeable football fan and he proceeds to give them both some well-founded advice on the goal-scoring tactics of the Czech team. Facetiously Crisp suggests committing a foul against a new member of the Czech football team. (In Scene 6 we learn that the foul has indeed been committed and that Anderson's advice had not, alas, been taken seriously.) McKendrick joins them from his room on the third floor, and recognising Crisp and Broadbent from the previous day, he proceeds to address them under the continued misconception that they are philosophers, which again provides a touch of comedy.

This is a connecting scene in that the themes raised by the football match and the themes raised by the presence of the philosophers in Czechoslovakia are now intermingled in the action. We know that

Anderson will be off to see the football match in the afternoon, and the title of play, together with Crisp's comment, makes us feel that all will not be well—we have now been made to expect notable events of some kind.

NOTES AND GLOSSARY:

You didn't pull her, then?: a vulgar idiom for having sexual intercourse

UFA Cup: actually U.E.F.A., the Union of European Football Associations, which, apart from two annual competitions, holds the European Championships every four years in rotation with the World Cup

Hegel: Georg Wilhelm Friedrich Hegel (1770–1831), a German philosopher of great influence in the nineteenth century. His followers built on his idea that philosophy is the highest available form of knowledge and that all other branches of learning must be referred to it. They are divided into two groups: the Old Hegelians thought religion could be brought into harmony with philosophy, while the Young Hegelians saw philosophy as critical of religion. Marx was much influenced by a Young Hegelian, Ludwig Feuerbach (1804–72)

epistemological: pertaining to a branch of philosophy that investigates the origin, nature, method and limits of human knowledge

Positivists: those following the doctrine of philosophy put forward by Auguste Comte (1798–1857) and his followers, which asserts that knowledge of reality can be achieved only through empirical methods. Metaphysical propositions are rejected by positivism

Quine: Willard van Orman Quine (*b*. 1908), an American philosopher who has concerned himself largely with language and logic, but who has widened somewhat the ethical and metaphysical scope allowed by linguistic philosophy

Scene 5

It is still Saturday morning and the camera now takes us to the colloquium which is an elaborate affair with simultaneous translations of the lectures provided through earphones to the colloquium's participants. There are many people there; obviously it is a prestigious event for the host country. An American, Stone, is giving a lecture on ambiguity. It is Quinian in approach, that is, concerned with language and logic. There is a witty connection between the whispered conversation of Anderson and McKendrick and the lecture; there *was* unintentional ambiguity in Anderson's remarks about the footballers which could lead to McKendrick's misunderstanding of them as philosophers. Moreover hearing the lecturer put forward a fundamental division of language into 'logical language' and 'ordinary language' adds to the feeling of displacement that the play is conjuring up. What is this logical language which no-one uses except philosophers, and which cannot be used to express our needs and emotions? Analogously, what is this political doctrine that cannot accommodate the individual? Meanwhile McKendrick has learnt where Anderson is off to in the afternoon and the true identity of Crisp and Broadbent. When McKendrick gives Anderson a copy of his lecture, which Anderson will miss because of the match, Anderson opens his briefcase. Once again our attention is brought to this piece of hand luggage that contains the main stage prop, Hollar's thesis—the object of the main line of action in the play. Anderson broods over the thesis, as we the viewers do. What will be its fate? One thing becoming clearer to us, though we do not yet know if it is becoming clearer to Anderson, is that Anderson's private game of ethics or 'ethical fiction' with which he confronts reality cannot respond adequately to the extreme circumstances he has encountered in Czechoslovakia. But we do see that Anderson has by no means dismissed Hollar from his thoughts, and so the issue is still open. Will he really stick to his theory of good manners and contracts? Stoppard is enthralling the audience with the suspense of these uncertainties symbolised by a professor's briefcase and its contents. Is it the thesis and Hollar's appeal to him in the hotel room that have inspired his magnificently succinct summary of the weaknesses of linguistic philosophy which closes the scene? For when he rises to slip out of the colloquium to go to his football match via Hollar's flat, his rising is taken by the Chairman as meaning that he has a question to ask. This is another amusing ambiguity. He has not, of course, and McKendrick watches with relish to see how well Anderson will cope with the situation. He copes splendidly. It is not a question, but, as he says, an observation, an observation which is in fact one of the messages of the play: linguistic philosophy is on the wrong track, the crucial truths exist independently of language and are not complicated. Language often obscures this fact.

This scene offers examples of pointers which Stoppard places throughout the play indicating his final goal. We must take this goal to be the answer to the question: what constitutes moral behaviour, or what deviations in generally accepted moral behaviour are allowable when one is confronted by violations of intrinsic human rights? Scenes 1 and 2 in the play have mapped out the pitch, and in Scene 3 we have seen what the game is about. In Scene 4, the philosophical action is underpinned by the metaphor of a football game, and now in Scene 5 we are gradually shown how the various schools of philosophy might handle questions of ethics in a practical context. What Anderson's and McKendrick's involvements will be is not yet shown to us, but in this scene Stone exposes unwittingly the weaknesess of linguistic philosophy by showing the trivia of its objects of study—'John eats well' and so on—and the limitations of its application (much of what he says is untranslatable). But nevertheless Stone's speculation on the adverb 'well' does lead him to consider what constitutes sound theory: it should take account of the particular or the individual, even the unique and hypothetical, that is, a theory that is not flexible enough to accommodate the sum total of reality will be false in its limitations. This is to become part of the author's message. Chetwyn's contribution to the action, like Anderson's and McKendrick's, is not yet known to us the viewers, though his boredom is an indication of what it will be, as well as a clue to what our own reactions should be to Stone's philosophising. The scene ends strongly with Anderson's observation and points the play on in the direction of that observation, so that though the underlying arguments of the play are not yet clear to the viewer, he is nevertheless well on the way to grasping them.

At this point it is clear that at least seven of the scenes in the play end humorously, six of them with humour based on misunderstanding or talk at cross-purposes, and Scene 5 belongs to this category.

NOTES AND GLOSSARY:

idiomatic: peculiar to a particular idiom which can be (a) a language or dialect, or style of speaking, (b) an expression, the meaning of which cannot be derived from its constituent elements, as in *not turning a hair*, meaning 'to be unconcerned'

Match of the Day: a showing on television of a Saturday football match pre-selected as being of special interest and usually broadcast on Saturday evening or on Sunday, the day after the game

Broadway: a major street in New York where most of its theatres are located

fons et origo: (*Latin*) source and origin.

monolithic: literally, made of a single block of stone, like a monument made from a single block of stone, of considerable size. Its applied meaning is something of a uniform, massive and intractable quality

Scene 6

This scene is the longest in the play. Anderson arrives with the fateful briefcase early on the Saturday afternoon at a rather squalid block of old-fashioned flats. He rings the bell at Hollar's front door, only to find it opened by a strange man. A scene of confusion starts to build up, more confusing for Anderson than for the viewer who is given the benefit of subtitles for the Czech-speaking characters. The viewer therefore understands almost immediately that the many men who quickly come into view are plain-clothes policemen (Mrs Hollar says in Czech that Pavel has been arrested), whereas Anderson takes a while to realise what is going on. He reacts with fear and with an instinct for self-preservation in this scene, trying to use his status as professor and foreign guest of the government to extricate himself from the situation and to get to the football match on time. However, he is detained against his will. He does not understand that Mrs Hollar would like him to be her witness for the search, a legal right which is being denied to her by the police. Despite the confusion caused by the number of policemen and the language problem, nevertheless certain details of daily life in this totalitarian state become apparent. The flat, built for one family, is in fact shared by three households. It is being searched with paranoic meticulousness—a kind of physical inquisition. Little respect is paid to individuals' legal rights—for example, Anderson's wallet is taken from him—let alone human consideration. When it is understood that he has a ticket for the match, no effort is made to arrange matters so that he can see the game. However, the police allow the radio to be played, but this, of course, is a dramatic expedient as much as anything, for thereby we learn of Broadbent's professional foul. Indeed at that point the radio, having served its purpose, is turned off. Meanwhile the police captain arrives. Anderson attempts to persuade him to let him go on the grounds of his status, and, rather ignobly, on the grounds that the whole situation and the Hollar family are of no interest to him. But the police captain has been well trained in interrogation techniques. Every statement Anderson makes is twisted to put him in a weaker position, and though Anderson never becomes Mrs Hollar's witness, his detention at the flat is justified for that reason. The captain's tactics are clearly exposed when he leads Anderson into making remarks about Hollar. These remarks allow the captain to criticise Hollar on the grounds of his having been a student abroad, but his critical conclusion to the argument is not Hollar's ideological contamination (for the Czech constitution does not allow that), but it is on criminal grounds. When the authorities cannot prosecute dissidents *legally*, they simply manufacture evidence for legal criminal charges. (A parallel situation in real life occurred with Stoppard's Czech contemporary, the playwright Vaclav Havel.) Hollar was arrested before the incriminating evidence was found, presumably because his contact with Anderson at the hotel was seen as the last straw by the authorities. We then hear of Broadbent's foul, and Anderson gets up to leave. Again the police captain leads Anderson into a conversation that seemingly exposes him as the carrier of Hollar's thesis. But Anderson deftly lies himself out of the situation (another minor 'professional foul') and produces instead from his briefcase the transcripts of his and McKendrick's papers which he says he has promised to give to Hollar. It is on this occasion that we learn the title of McKendrick's talk: 'Philosophy and the Catastrophe Theory' (see Commentary, Part 3, p.44). The scene ends with the 'discovery' of foreign currency under the floorboards, the major 'foul' of the play, following shortly after the foul of the football match. Anderson departs in the midst of the confusion, leaving Mrs Hollar to be comforted by her little son Sacha.

NOTES AND GLOSSARY:

J.S. Mill: (1806–73), one of Britain's greatest nineteenth-century thinkers, wrote on economics and philosophy (where he was much influenced by Locke), including the rights of individuals, socialist theory, utilitarianism and the equality of the sexes

black market: a market where illegal buying and selling of goods takes place, normally set up in times of hardship or when there is strict government control of some commodity

hard currency: in this context any Western currency

professional foul: a violation of the rules of football specifically committed in order to prevent the scoring of a goal. Broadbent's foul was 'to scythe Deml down from behind', that is, Broadbent tripped Deml up just before he tried for a goal

Catastrophe Theory: defined by McKendrick in Scene 8. The theory is based on analogies with topological forms, that is, if a system depends on two or more factors, a particular state of the system can be represented by a point in three-dimensional space, and the system being represented by the shape of the plane. A certain point or points on the plane can represent a catastrophic state in the system where a radical change or a collapse might occur, for example, the factors represented by the plane could be various engineering conditions for a bridge. In our case,

there is a point in the unresponsive pursuit of an
ethic where it could actually have the opposite
effect on its goal—Chetwyn's behaviour might be
an example of this, or the Czech state's arrest of
Hollar, who will no doubt receive more publicity
for his ideas now than he would have done otherwise

Scene 7

Early on the Saturday evening, Anderson returns to his hotel room
worn out. Fumbling with his key in the lock, he hears the voice of his
neighbour in the room next door. It is obvious he is a journalist dictating his account of the football match over the telephone to his British
paper. Anderson invites himself in to listen as a substitute for the game
he missed. It seems that Czechoslovakia beat England 4−0. Both Grayson and Chamberlain provide Stoppard with a splendid opportunity to
parody journalism as Grayson's extravagant banking metaphor shows,
starting off with the pun 'bouncing Czechs', and so forth. Anderson
has his theory about the well-prepared tactics or set piece of the Czech
game confirmed, as well as the foul committed by Broadbent. Having
heard enough, Anderson slips away.

NOTES AND GLOSSARY:

Czechs bouncing: pun on a 'bouncing cheque', that is, a cheque
returned by the bank to the creditor without pay-
ment as the debtor has emptied his bank account.
Stoppard is generally very fond of using puns (as
we see in his plays, notably in *Jumpers* and *Travesties*), though there are not many in this play. It
could be argued that they are an extension of the
dialectical, that is, argumentative style of his plays
in so far as puns depend on a kind of argument:
their double meaning. His conversations at cross-
purposes are a kind of extended pun, and there are
many examples of these in this play.

bankruptcy: not having enough cash to settle debts when
required, so that creditors can demand that all the
debtor's non-cash assets should be sold in order to
meet at least part of the debts

go round the halls as a telepathy act: tour provincial theatres or music
halls with a double act (an act with two actors)
which entertains using (mock) telepathy (mind
reading)

Madame Tussaud's: the famous waxworks museum in London, founded in the early nineteenth century by Marie Tussaud (1761–1850). It contains realistic wax effigies of famous people, past and present

salt and vinegar flavoured: a pun on the name Crisp, which is also a word for a potato snack that can be bought in various flavours including salt and vinegar. Here it means that Crisp's comment was sour and 'salted' with oaths

Scene 8

It is Saturday evening after dinner in the hotel dining-room. Stone, the American philosopher, a Frenchman, Anderson, McKendrick and Chetwyn are sharing a table. It is obvious from their expressions that our three English protagonists are subdued, whereas Stone and the Frenchman are having a lively conversation. In fact at least three conversations are taking place and two of them consist of unanswered questions or are at cross-purposes. Stone and the Frenchman are arguing a point of linguistic philosophy, McKendrick is morosely lustful, and Chetwyn is considering the rarity of having goose on the menu. McKendrick finally joins in by making a joke at the expense of linguistic philosophy and Stone's eating habits. This reminds us what good manners really mean as opposed to ethical behaviour, and it puts Anderson's objection to Hollar's plea in Scene 3 in its place. Stone and the Frenchman conveniently depart, leaving the three Englishmen in front of the camera. The scene that follows firstly establishes that Chetwyn absented himself from the afternoon at the colloquium for unstated but guessable purposes ('I have friends here, that's all'). Secondly, Anderson's absence from the match allows McKendrick to speculate about Anderson's possible involvement in a love afair and crudely misunderstand his meeting with Mrs Hollar at the end of the scene. And, thirdly, McKendrick explains the catastrophe theory, that is, that morality is not a simple linear progression (see also explanation on page 35), and in so doing, unwittingly manages to touch a sore point in Anderson's conscience, for Anderson gets uncharacteristically annoyed. At this point the crumbling of his 'ethical fiction', the fortress of narrow rules he has allowed himself to construct to cope with reality, becomes apparent. And of course, Anderson's annoyance also reflects the inherent weakness of the catastrophe theory—it could be abused so as to become the worst kind of utilitarianism, but that is not the true meaning of it. For principles are not actually systems, they are the total of what 'principled' or morally searching individuals are trying to act out.

This is a turning point in the play. Unknown to himself McKendrick is providing the philosophical justification for the action that Anderson has so far felt unable to undertake: the smuggling out of Hollar's thesis. And Chetwyn adds weight to Hollar's argument that inherent rights are so intelligible that a child can see them, for he too refers to his eight-year-old son when moral problems seem complex. By Anderson's response we can conclude that the coincidence does not go unnoticed by him. McKendrick draws attention to a woman waiting in the vestibule, and when Anderson sees it is Mrs Hollar he leaves to speak to her, conspicuously taking his briefcase with him.

NOTES AND GLOSSARY:

Dickens:	Charles Dickens (1812–70), English novelist who began his writing career by contributing monthly instalments of his stories to popular magazines. He achieved fame with *The Pickwick Papers* in 1837. His works depict the destructive powers of money and ambition, and contain many colourful and memorable caricatures of characters found in the unjust society of nineteenth-century England
brewing up:	making tea

Scene 9

This moving scene marks the second meeting of Anderson and Mrs Hollar and the complete change in his attitude. His immediate and unforced response to her presence at the end of the previous scene is yet another of the small changes in his disposition that reveal his mental and moral progress through the play. Anderson and Mrs Hollar walk towards a bench in a park where Sacha is sitting. Sacha has to interpret in his broken and elementary English. The main purpose of their seeking out Anderson is to ensure the safety of the thesis. But meanwhile we hear the usual catalogue of the horrors that befall dissidents: Pavel Hollar was indeed arrested outside the hotel after visiting Anderson (contact with foreigners is discouraged, and in the case of dissidents, virtually forbidden); the police searched the Hollar flat throughout the Friday night until 7.00 p.m. on the Saturday; the police planted the dollars; the Hollars are under constant surveillance; and so far they have been refused access to Pavel in the cells. The main cause for these troubles was his signing a letter to Husak. Then we witness the fundamental change in Anderson's attitude. Sacha asks for the return of his father's thesis, and Anderson replies that he has been asked to take it to England, implying that this is what he will do. However, Sacha points out that Anderson is now liable to be searched. Anderson responds by treating Sacha as an adult confidant and begins to apologise for his behaviour and his previous lack of comprehension of the situation in Czechoslovakia. Sacha, of course, does not understand. But we begin to understand that Anderson is a man who defends himself because he would otherwise be too much moved by the troubles and misfortunes of life. Small, brave boys who have fathers in prison must be safely translated into adults. As part of a philosophical theory, as the previous scene showed, the concepts of innocence, youth, and vulnerability are understood, but living with them is not so easy. Anderson indicates his willingness to do whatever they wish, and Sacha asks him to hand the thesis to a friend of theirs, Jan, at the colloquium the next day. Anderson promises to help Pavel in any way he can from England, and when Sacha starts to cry, continues with his adult reassurances. However, the childish tears surprise him, and he is brought to realise the mistake his defences cause him to make. The scene ends with his honourable statement that he will do everything he can for Hollar.

NOTES AND GLOSSARY:

He is signing something: the letter to Husak, first referred to in Scene 3, could be what Sacha means here. It could also be a reference to Charter 77. One of Sacha's main mistakes in his English is his constant use of the present continuous tense, a tense rarely used by native English speakers

Scene 10

It is late on Saturday night. With the aid of the wandering eye of the television camera we are able to follow Anderson from his room, where he has been lying fully dressed on his bed thinking about the situation, to Grayson's room. No doubt the faint voices coming from his neighbour's room help to arouse him to action. He asks Grayson at his door if he may borrow his typewriter until the morning. It is not until the next scene that the use of the typewriter will be fully explained. McKendrick is in Grayson's room, together with the footballers Crisp and Broadbent, and Chamberlain, the second journalist. The first drunken words we hear from McKendrick are undoubtedly proving to be true: 'You'll do well to listen to what I have to say'. Anderson enters with the intention of persuading McKendrick to leave, as he is annoying the footballers' wounded pride. But McKendrick continues to hold forth, and in so doing makes it clear to us where the parallel between the football match and the main action of the play breaks down.

The football match is far from a perfect allegory; it functions as an intermittent metaphor, of pertinence in certain aspects only. For, as

UBERTON HIGH SCHOOL

McKendrick implies, the whole ethos of the football game is fundamentally different from the whole ethos of life. The whole ethos of the game is *not* to cheat and to succeed skilfully within the rules, and thus a foul is not tolerable, whereas the whole ethos of life in Czechoslovakia *is* so foul that the committing of one small foul in order to lessen the suffering with a little hope, is no crime at all. And this is no charter for utilitarianism, because such acts of expediency are only permissible in a catastrophic situation. (McKendrick's speech in Scene 10 has been combined in this summing up with his speech at the dinner table in Scene 8.) The rest of his tipsy talk is confined more specifically to the nature of football and constitutes a pretty devastating criticism of the players and spectators of the game.

He reverts to a class-conscious analysis of the three major forms of British sport, namely soccer, rugger and cricket, and, to put it simply, places himself on the middle tier as a follower of rugger, Anderson on the top tier as a cricketer (which is not actually the case; Anderson is a soccer fan, but the classification works metaphorically), and the 'yobs' on the bottom tier with football. Anderson's sharp little comment which is intended to sober him up, is not quite fair. McKendrick, for all his crudity, is no mere pragmatist. His philosophical theory is sound, sounder, it seems, than his social behaviour. His conclusion that football seems to attract 'yobs' is at last too much for Broadbent who punches him in the face. Anderson's charitable act of helping the dazed and drunk McKendrick back to his room, offers him a way of smuggling out Hollar's thesis, though this is not yet known to the viewer.

NOTES AND GLOSSARY:

soccer:	association football. The game has two teams of eleven players; the ball may be advanced only by kicking it or bouncing it off the body, not using arms and hands. Only goalkeepers may use their hands. The most popular game in Britain
rugger:	Rugby football. There are two teams of up to fifteen players a side; the ball is oval and may be kicked or passed by hand. It is a game, generally speaking, that has in the past been more associated with public schools than with state-aided education
left winger:	a pun. It is a loose term for the position of a player in football, as well as a term for a person with left-wing, or socialist, political tendencies
yob:	an uncouth, uneducated, and unprincipled youth
They don't teach you nothing at that place then:	a rather confusing remark. He probably means: 'I haven't been properly prepared in the English Team's headquarters for the game'. 'You' probably means 'one' or 'me'

Scene 11

It is now Sunday morning, the morning of Anderson's lecture to the philosophical colloquium. We see Anderson coming to the lectern with a bundle of type-written papers. We are about to realise that during the night he rewrote his lecture on Grayson's typewriter. His lecture is on the same topic as Hollar's thesis and makes quite clear references to violations of human rights of the kind that Hollar himself has suffered. The Chairman, we see, acts as a censor and attempts to stop Anderson from speaking on this topic. But Anderson wins the argument, for the Chairman, and, for that matter, the Czech state, does not like to be seen publicly violating the constitution, which guarantees human rights. He therefore has to resort to subterfuge. The Chairman seeks advice behind the scenes, and as we learn in Scene 14, is told to raise a false fire alarm to clear the hall. Meanwhile Anderson continues, and his argument is along these lines: There are three senses is which human beings could be said to have rights, (i) if they collectively agree to give each other certain rights, but this is too limiting, that is, it becomes a matter of rules rather than of ethics and is therefore discountable, (ii) if it is believed that rights are endowed by God, or (iii) if we decide to define rights as ethical fictions that have the status of truth. (This last is Anderson's own view.) The interesting thing is the degree of consensus on the idea of human rights, no matter what their ethical origin. Thus the Christian-based American constitution is remarkably similar to the atheist Czechoslovak constitution. This points us in the direction of discovering some fundamental human values.

NOTES AND GLOSSARY:

American Founding Fathers: the delegates to the Convention in Philadelphia in 1787 who agreed on the American Constitution

Constitution: the system of fundamental principles or laws according to which a nation is governed

Scene 12

While Anderson is still lecturing, the camera takes us to McKendrick's room where we see him recovering from a severe hangover. We see his half-packed (or was it never unpacked?) luggage including his brief-case. His watch has stopped, so he telephones Anderson to find out the time.

Scene 13

We are shown the telephone in Anderson's room and hear it ring, but then the camera widens its focus to include two plain-clothes policemen who are meticulously searching the room without disturbing anything. The phone goes on ringing unanswered.

Scene 14

We return to the colloquium and Anderson's lecture. Anderson describes the stance of linguistic philosophy in relation to ethics, that is, that 'ethics are not the inspiration of our behavior but merely the creation of our utterances'. He proceeds to demolish this, artfully using the arguments of Chetwyn and Hollar that a child would know the difference. There is, he says: 'a sense of right and wrong which precedes utterance. It is individually experienced and it concerns one person's dealings with another person. From this experience we have built a system of ethics which is the sum of individual acts of recognition of individual right.' Thus a State which seeks to suppress individual rights, is suppressing the very individuals who compose the State. The stock criticism of this view, that it is 'bourgeois logic' makes no sense; it is a mere label, for logic, like any subject with its own stringent rules, has nothing to do with social class. At this point the fire alarm rings, all the philosophers have to leave the hall, including Anderson, who takes it all very calmly. He has had his say.

NOTES AND GLOSSARY:

Eiffel Tower:	a metal tower in Paris built for the 1889 exhibition. It was the design of Alexandre-Gustave Eiffel (1832–1923), and until 1930 was the highest building in the world
platonic:	Plato (429–347BC), Greek philosopher and disciple of Socrates, best known for his theory of forms which held that the world is a feeble and imperfect copy of perfect spiritual entities. He was disillusioned by both democratic and aristocratic rule and advocated a utopian state run by philosopher kings

Scene 15

It is now Sunday afternoon and we are at the airport. We see the departing passengers' luggage being carefully searched, especially Anderson's. Even a cellophane-wrapped box of chocolates is opened and examined, and so on. McKendrick, at another bench, escapes with only a perfunctory look. But Chetwyn is being submitted to the same detailed search as Anderson. The customs man sees a bulge in the zipped compartment on the underside of the lid of Anderson's suitcase. To us, the viewers, it looks very much like something the size and shape of Hollar's thesis. It turns out, however, that it is nothing other than McKendrick's sex magazine. Back to Chetwyn, we see that some hidden papers (probably letters to Amnesty International and the U.N.) have been discovered. Chetwyn is white with fear.

Scene 16

The play ends as it started: in the aeroplane. McKendrick and Anderson are sitting together. Chetwyn has been detained, and they discuss his fate. Anderson feels sure that Chetwyn will be put on the next plane to England. Anderson gives a pragmatic answer to McKendrick's question of whether he would have smuggled something out: 'No. He should have known he'd be searched'. Anderson then takes the opportunity to reveal that he hid Hollar's thesis in McKendrick's briefcase on Saturday night, and justifies his action by referring to McKendrick's catastrophe theory, 'I'm afraid I reversed a principle'. McKendrick was unlikely to be searched. Shocked and angry, McKendrick is unmoved by the philosophical reference, and refers, ironically enough, to the rules of the social game, rather as Anderson himself did to Hollar in Scene 3. But such rules are more appropriate to football than to the complexities of life. He has forgotten that there is 'the whole *ethos*' to consider. But Anderson lightly concedes that McKendrick may have a point. It is all very complicated, and that is what philosophical congresses are for: to sort out what constitutes ethical behaviour. The plane and Hollar's thesis take off for England.

NOTES AND GLOSSARY:

Amnesty International: founded in Britain in 1961 by Peter Benenson. It aims to defend freedom of speech and religion in all parts of the world, and campaigns for the release of 'prisoners of conscience'. It has bases in seventy-five countries

U.N.: United Nations, founded in 1945. An organisation established to maintain international peace and to foster international co-operation for the resolution of economic, social and humanitarian problems. Most countries of the world are now members of the U.N.

Part 3

Commentary

Professional Foul is quite unlike Stoppard's pre-1977 plays written for the stage. It is constructed as a simple, realistic story, told chronologically. The action begins one Friday lunch-time, and ends the following Sunday afternoon. There are no flashbacks, the development is linear, and the camera stays with the main protagonist Anderson throughout (except when it cuts to McKendrick and his room very briefly on the Sunday morning). Some aspects of the play could almost come from one of the more straightforward witnesses' accounts from the archives of Amnesty International. Indeed some of the meticulously reported detail of the Hollars' living conditions and the circumstances surrounding Pavel's arrest are obviously influenced by Amnesty material. So, on the one hand, the play is a kind of reportage, particularly appropriate for Prisoner of Conscience Year (1977) for which television is so suitable a medium. On the other hand, there are several more layers in the play. Most obviously the play is itself a fairly complicated philosophical debate about what constitutes ethical behaviour in the face of totalitarianism. The complexity here lies in the diverse schools of thought which are used piecemeal to build up to Anderson's change of mind and his concluding action. As an extra layer, there is the appended story of the football game, used metaphorically as well as directly in the philosophical argument. The metaphor is a device which can simplify the understanding of the philosophical issues. It allows half-perceived notions of 'playing the game', what is appropriate on the field and what off it (that is, in human behaviour), to carry the viewer through the more abstract aspects of the play so that he does not lose touch and therefore sympathy with Anderson and his actions. But in comparison with the complexities of *Jumpers* and *Travesties*, *Professional Foul* seems nevertheless relatively straightforward. It certainly has fewer complications in its use of language; its range of reference is more or less left within the confines of philosophy, contemporary human rights issues in the Soviet bloc and to some extent sport. There are no games played with literary or historical characters, and only very little pastiche.

Thus we have a topical story and a philosophical debate. But lastly, we also have a portrait of a man undergoing a change of heart. The character of Anderson, who is always in front of our eyes, is of major importance in the play, and his development comes to rival the interest of the sparring ideas.

As we get to know a work of literature, various topics and questions present themselves as worthy of more detailed consideration. A list of such questions, which will be discussed in this part of the Notes, is given below. You too should, of course, make similar lists of your own. You may arrive at more interesting topics to consider than those suggested here. The main thing is to read actively, and to set about solving any seeming enigmas primarily from the information contained in the text itself. Do not read this part of the Notes without first reading the play and Part 2, Summaries.

Topics for the Commentary:

(i)   In what way is this play specifically television drama?
(ii) How does the dramatic action unfold?
(iii) What makes this play characteristically Stoppardian?
(iv) What are the philosophical themes?
(v)   What are the 'professional fouls'?
(vi) How are the characters drawn?

In what way is this play specifically television drama?

Television differs from the stage. There is certainly loss of spontaneity on television with the absence of a live performance, and the absence of feedback from a live audience. But the camera allows for pre-recording techniques and therefore gives much greater scope in the choice of settings. This in turn can lead to a far greater flexibility in the dramatic structure of television plays through montage and editing; rapid shifts in time, place—from realistic worlds to fantastic worlds—can occur within seconds. Because of the flexibility and intimacy of the camera, television presents a more convincing illusion of reality. However, large, subtly orchestrated scenes as found in some nineteenth-century plays (those of the Russian dramatist Anton Chekhov (1860–1904) in particular) contain too much for the intimate eye of the camera. We should also remember that television is shown in the intimate surroundings of people's homes, and that this too, as well as the scope and limitations of the medium, influences the forms of its drama.

In many ways, *Professional Foul* is a very typical television drama. It makes however, little use of the elaborate montage and editing techniques available. This presentation technique seems to be related to a generally accepted idea of the limitations of a mass audience, and it is none the less typical for that. To quote Stoppard:

Television in theory is one thing and television in practice is another. As a medium it is flexible, but in practice the television set-up is such that in most cases a space is looking for a particular thing to fill it. Television likes to have things with an air of continuity; therefore there has turned out to be a sort of code suggesting a certain atmosphere, that the audience will be able to identify with at least one and possibly all the characters in a television play. This isn't always necessary or desirable with stage plays.*

Though written almost ten years before *Professional Foul* these words still seem to apply to the play. The characters are certainly depicted in a clearly identifiable way; in some respects they have caricature traits. The action is certainly neither as complicated nor as fantastic as in *Jumpers* or *Travesties*; nor is there the complication of time shifts as in *Travesties*. It seems that expectations of theatre audiences can override technical limitations on the stage, but notions of television audiences' expectations prevent the full use of the readily available possibilities of television. But to what advantage Stoppard puts the television's capacity for creating realistic situations! The audience is artfully but firmly guided to the moral conflict that Anderson encounters in Czechoslovakia. Each moral argument is represented by an appropriate and recognisable character, or housed in an appropriate situation; and each criticism of totalitarianism is made by empirical evidence, that is, by situations that we observe, and not by political theorising or bombast. Thus we are spectators of the Hollars' sufferings and we experience the arguments of the play through the characters.

It then follows that the language of the play, the words the characters speak, must be realistic too. And so it is, without losing subtlety. But while Stoppard's stage plays also employ such elaborate word games as parody, pastiche and puns to enhance the overall meaning of the play, *Professional Foul* relies more on accurate representations of modes of speech, carefully engineered situations, structured conversations, and one or two physical or visual symbols. The philosophical references are strictly confined to those that build up the philosophical issue raised by the play; significant character traits—for example, Anderson's anxiety and fastidiousness—are conveyed by a tight economy in his choice of words: not a line is out of character. Similarly McKendrick is drawn with unrelenting consistency; not for one moment are we left in doubt that he is as unsound in his social behaviour as he is sound in his grasp of theoretical ethics. Unlike the cheerful word games in Stoppard's previous works, the puns in this play are parallel metaphors: the cross-purpose conversations that emphasise a feeling of displacement, the football game, and the fouls committed by

* Tom Stoppard, 'Something to Declare', *The Sunday Times*, 25 February 1968.

several of the characters—Broadbent, the police, Anderson. The main engineered situation is the literal confrontation of ethics and totalitarian politics made by setting the play at a philosophical colloquium in Prague. And the main visual symbol that helps us to focus on the action is the briefcase which we follow anxiously on its journey throughout the play.

Realistic language extends to Czech-speaking actors, which again helps to transport us to the very scene of the action without any loss of comprehensibility, as we have, as television viewers, the facility of subtitles.

Lastly, there must be the topicality. *Professional Foul* was written to commemorate and publicise the year of the Prisoner of Conscience. Its topic and setting refer to the then much publicised Czech troubles and Charter 77. Using television, the issues were put before a large audience, and obviously, Stoppard intended to hold this audience. He used many devices to do so, especially those of suspense and simplicity of plot. When writing for the stage, on the other hand, he seems to be writing much more for his own entertainment, making experiments in staging and airing his epistomological musings in public. These plays have certainly been more fantastic and extravagant than his television works, including *Professional Foul*.

How does the dramatic action unfold?

As part of his television strategy, the action of the play contains an unusual amount of suspense for Stoppard. Consider the inaction of *Rosencrantz*, the muddle of *Jumpers* (George Moore fails to do anything); in *Travesties*, too, there is not so much action as presentation of ideas. But in *Professional Foul* the excitement and anticipation start from Scene 1, where we are kept teasingly in suspense about Anderson's 'ulterior motive', mysteriously mentioned there and equally mysteriously hinted at in the passing over of an envelope in Scene 2. In Scene 3 the real suspense starts with the atmosphere of menace that Hollar brings with him from the totalitarian world outside the hotel and with his handing over of the thesis to Anderson. From that moment, we scarcely ever lose sight of it in Anderson's briefcase, and its presence and its fate are kept in our minds by little highlighting devices such as the police captain's interest in its contents (Scene 6) and Anderson's forgetting it under the table (Scene 8).

Each scene has components that drive the arguments and the action of the play forward. For instance, Scene 1 takes us forward with the contrasts of interests and character between Anderson and McKendrick, the latter of whom is to be both the agent and victim of the action. Scenes 2 and 4 involve the action with the football match. Scene 3 introduces the thesis, Scene 5 the presentation of the philosophical issues. Scene 6 confronts Anderson with Czech authorities and threatens the content of the briefcase, and so on. At the play's philosophical climax, when Anderson delivers his lecture, we are again in double suspense as to whether he will be able to have his say before he is driven off the stage and whether in the meantime the police will have found anything in his room. We are allowed to believe until the very end that Anderson is probably smuggling the thesis out in his brie_fcase, and when he escapes from the customs and calmly collects it from McKendrick in the aeroplane, this comes as a surprise on the screen. The suspense, the twist, the significance of one or two props—these are good standard components of popular drama.

Interestingly, Aristotle is mentioned (in Scene 2, though Anderson's remark to Chetwyn is of no direct relevance to the action of our tragicomedy). In his *Poetics*, apart from stating that tragedy properly dealt with the fall of the great, Aristotle also stated that plot or action is more important than characterisation (a view which Stoppard seems to hold himself) and that a good plot has various elements, reversal, discovery and calamity. In the simple chronology of the play, there are many such Aristotelian turning-points, though here perhaps better described as confrontations. Basically, the play is a confrontation between philosophy and politics—the colloquium in Prague. More specifically, Anderson confronts a workable ethic in the conversation with McKendrick, most noticeably in Scene 8 (the dinner on Saturday evening) and Scene 10 (in Grayson's room with the footballers late Saturday night). He confronts the main problem of the play, and we realise thereby his ethical limitations, in Scene 3 when Hollar comes to him with his thesis, and again in Scene 6 at the flat when the full frightening extent of the problem is revealed. What could be termed the reversal occurs after a combination of circumstances have made their effect on Anderson: the police at the flat, McKendrick's catastrophe theory, the footballer's foul plus the pathos of the night-time meeting with Mrs Hollar and Sacha (Scene 9). Then his decision about what to do with the thesis 'reverses' and so does the content of his lecture for the colloquium. It would be true to say that the action is a process of discovery: self-discovery for Anderson, and a discovery for both him and the viewers of the illogicality and repressive nature of the government in Czechoslovakia. The whole plot of course gains momentum through the calamity of the individual, Hollar, in this totalitarian regime.

This is not to say that the play is consciously Aristotelian, but merely to point out that it certainly contains Aristotelian confrontations which give the action its character and strength.

What makes this play characteristically Stoppardian?

As we can see from Part 1 of these Notes, Stoppard's drama contains certain characteristic devices. Though *Professional Foul*, as a TV play, is a modified form of his drama, it is nevertheless recognisable as Stoppardian. These devices could be listed as

(a) contrasts of mood
(b) humour: wit (including punning, mistaken identity and pastiche) and farce
(c) seriousness of theme
(d) philosophical argument

The play has marked changes of mood, which makes the label 'tragi-comedy' seem not unhelpful. The action develops through scenes of witty and light conversation (Scenes 1 and 2) to scenes of horror and pathos (Scenes 3, 6 and 9), scenes of philosophising of staggering irrelevance (Scene 5), or cheerful pastiche (both of philosophers and of journalists), and a drunken gathering (Scene 10). But the high point of the play is a definition of human rights which is juxtaposed with McKendrick's hangover and a secret police search. These contrasts are, on the one hand, the very stuff of life, and, on the other hand, a tamer version of the curious contrasts that Stoppard creates in *Jumpers* and *Travesties*. In the latter play Lenin stands out as a humourless historical portrayal amid the travesties of Carr's caricatures of Joyce and Tzara, and of Oscar Wilde's play. George Moore in *Jumpers* philosophises in his study while the nation undergoes a *coup d'état* and his wife harbours a murdered man and entertains the new prime minister in the bedroom. But while McKendrick, Anderson and the other Western philosophers provide a contrast with a repressed nation, which forms the basis for the changes of mood in the play, their presence is of course highly apposite: they provide a yardstick against which the actions of the Czech state can be measured. It is a clever and witty choice of situation.

The second Stoppardian quality is the humour. *Professional Foul* lacks the farce which is the usual stamp of his comedy, though the economy of the action seems to come from a writer skilled in manipulating plots. There are probably only two elements of farce, if we discount the illogicality of totalitarianism: the two inappropriate appearances of the girly magazine and the ringing of the fire bell. The humour comes chiefly, and typically, from verbal high spirits, again more subdued than before, but nevertheless identifiable in all their Stoppardian forms: mistaken identity, talk at cross-purposes, puns, pastiche, visual humour and situation comedy. The tenor of the play, despite its darker scenes, is high-spirited and good-humoured.

Mistaken identity is a very old trick of plot. The *Oedipus Rex* of the Athenian dramatist Sophocles (469–399BC) comes first to mind, Shakespeare's comedies next, the commedia dell'arte,* and so on. But it has other than formal and traditional origins. It is also a symbol of our existential plight, the difficulty of knowing ourselves, and is therefore assured of a permanent place in drama. In Stoppard it takes one of its lighter forms in McKendrick's mistaking the footballers for philosophers, yet it also extends into political and social commentary as explained in Part 2, Summaries, p.27. Closely linked in both style and purpose are the misunderstandings in conversation—a kind of extended pun, either based directly on words (for example, 'left wing' and 'centre' in Scene 2) or on ideas (for example, Marxists as 'prudes', meaning both political purity and sexual purity in Scene 1).

There are few puns as such in this realistic play, though they are much used in Stoppard's earlier comedies. Such visual humour as there is, however, could also be seen as an extended pun of the mistaken identity type: the girly magazine that becomes a brochure for a philosophical colloquium or a dissident thesis: the journalist who looks like an East European spy. The basis of these humorous forms embodies a kind of dialectic, that is, puns seem to be language arguing with itself, and they are an apt reflection on Stoppard's style of self-argument which is to be found in his plays.

The pastiche (see Notes and Glossary, p.18) covers donnish conversations, philosophical lectures and journalese. It is subdued enough to be realistic and only now and again verges on the humorous. When it does so, it depends as much on the situation as upon the actual content. Thus it is the contrast of Anderson's and McKendrick's whispers with Stone's lecture that is mildly funny (Scene 5) and again, the contrasts of the non-communicating utterances at the dinner table (Scene 8) are funny rather than the utterances themselves. It could indeed be argued that the whole action and a lot of the accidental but humorous incongruities arise from the odd situation (not quite television situation comedy, but coming quite close to it) of the concurrence of a philosophical colloquium and a football match in Czechoslovakia. But if this play relies far less on deliberate joke-making than Stoppard's previous plays, it still displays his remarkable lightness of touch. The seriousness of its theme is well camouflaged by the humorous cross-

---

* Commedia dell'arte is the name given to popular improvised comedy which flourished in Italy in the sixteenth to eighteenth century. Each actor in the company played one character, for instance the old man, the pedant, the soldier, the maid, and so on, and played nothing else. Sometimes the actors wore stylised masks representing these stock characters. The commedia dell'arte exercised a considerable influence on European theatre generally, including the English pantomime as well as the French literary play, and on character acting in particular.

purpose exchanges and the fine observations of character that represent a new development in Stoppard's dramatic writing.

What are the philosophical themes?

As was indicated above, a characteristic quality of a Stoppard play is its blend of the humorous with serious philosophical argument. In *Professional Foul* the latter comes to the fore. There is no doubt that the play is carefully constructed to present a dialogue between current schools of philosophical thought in Britain. This dialogue is not literal —the different ideas are presented to us gradually (mostly in ways secondary to the action), and the contrast between them is telling. McKendrick represents 'applied' philosophy, that aspect of the subject which borrows the catastrophe theory from René Thom (*b*. 1923)* and uses it in considering practical problems in various fields of study, in McKendrick's case, sociology. Stone represents Quinian linguistic philosophy and its positivist limitations; Chetwyn Aristotelianism plus deism.† Anderson seems to be a mainstream philsopher, not seriously limited by linguistics, nor so new-fangled as to consider applications from other fields of study, nor part of a recent fashion for traditional Aristotelian ethics.

The situation is not easy to understand without some background knowledge of British philosophy. Stoppard does offer some help in forms of little clues dropped in the text (for example, Chetwyn's boredom in Scene 5) and, conveniently for the viewers, each philosopher always manages to encapsulate in quite straightforward language the essence of his position in the debate about human rights, even though none of them, except Chetwyn and Anderson later on, is directly concerned with the question. But the assumption that his audience is knowledgeable is typically Stoppardian; the only concessions to the viewers in *Professional Foul* are that there are no literary and historical allusions as well, and that, for those without the necessary philosophical knowledge, the play still makes clear sense. The metaphor or parable of the football match helps the viewer to find the ethical meaning.

We can use the football match to clarify the meaning of the play by regarding the central question as if set out on a metaphorical football pitch. The two goals are, on the one hand, the establishment of individual human rights and, on the other hand, the establishment of a collective ethic, that is, the paramount right of the state. The players are on

---

* René Thom is a French mathematician who developed the catastrophe theory in 1972.
† Deism is a belief in God, particularly strong in the eighteenth century, which is based on the idea of its own inherent reasonableness so that it needs no support from divine revelations or religious institutions. It is often understood as a belief that God left the universe to its own devices once the process of creation had been completed.

one side a team of philosophers of various schools of thought, on the other side a team of totalitarian politicians. The ball is the progress of the argument between the two goals. When the ball is passed to Stone, the Quinian linguistic philosopher, he dribbles it for a considerable length of time across the pitch in no purposeful direction, but then takes it off in the direction of the individual ethic, though not for long. As the play goes on to reveal, when the ball is passed to the impatient Chetwyn, the Aristotelian deist whose convictions are as strong as his tactics are unsubtle, he attempts to score from an inappropriate position in such a way as to invite the opposing team to tackle him and gain an advantage. This traditional and newly fashionable mixture of ethical philosophy and religion may be a direct route to the goal of human rights, but it is not the most appropriate, or at least, not the safest way there, considering the opposition. Anderson has no wish to be involved in the game and would prefer to remain a spectator, as he wanted to be in the real football game. But he is drawn in unwillingly by Hollar who has learnt his style of play from the democratic Paine and Locke. Then, when the low tactics of the opposing team have been made quite clear to Anderson (for example, Hollar is sent off wrongfully by a professional foul committed by the political team), he decides to set about scoring a victory for individual ethics by the most effective method available to him. This method could be described as 'opportunist' (an adjective applied to the footballer Broadbent in Scene 2) or utilitarian, and certainly not as respecting the rights of the individual McKendrick, the medium for Anderson's victory. But it could also be justified by the ingenious catastrophe theory expounded by McKendrick himself—in certain situations there comes a point on the plane of ethical behaviour where it must become like unethical behaviour if it is to continue to function ethically. If he were strictly to avoid the unethical in his method, it would in any case mean the abandonment of the original moral principle (see Scene 8). This is precisely the situation in which Anderson finds himself, and what is more, McKendrick is standing metaphorically on the side-line of the game shouting encouragement for the philosopher team and supporting the individual ethic with his catastrophe theory. Fundamentally a humane man, McKendrick is nevertheless so muddled by class-consciousness and a vulgar hedonism that he is not interested in actually playing the game. But Anderson has found him inspiring as well as a useful foil. He uses the unsuspecting McKendrick by skilfully kicking the ball at him (to continue with the metaphor), and it bounces off him into the goal, leaving him bruised, but not seriously injured. It is but a minor triumph in the seemingly endless game. The other side have also scored with the detention of Chetwyn, and Hollar is still imprisoned. It seems the team of totalitarian politicians is fated to win overall on home ground (as did the Czech football team); their control is too strong. But the play is not so much about who is winning or losing, but about *why* we should uphold the rights of individuals and *how* we might have to do so.

In terms of the philosophical theme, the climax of the play comes with Anderson's rewritten lecture for the colloquium. It is a succinct summary of the arguments for human rights, and, presumably, not unlike Hollar's thesis in its context. Conveniently, despite the interruption of the false fire alarm, Anderson manages to finish the outline of his case. He is really the mouthpiece for Stoppard's views, but not in any obvious way. He is more or less pushed into making the speech of Scenes 11 and 14 by key events in the action, and by his discriminating approval of the philosophical views gradually expressed during the weekend. The culminating view of human rights is one that is *achieved*, and by following Anderson's achievement, the viewer is in a better position to understand its value, in fact to feel won over to Anderson's and Stoppard's final points of view. The play is a clever piece of didacticism: seriousness tempered with good humour, and moving only gradually towards its conclusion with a clarifying parable or metaphor to ease the process of understanding.

There is no doubt that the whole movement of the philosophical argument also constitutes a critique of the current state of British philosophy. But it is not an indispensable part of the story. The tale of Hollar's thesis and the fastidious don who smuggles it out in the end is understandable without this dimension. So too is the idea that there are various kinds of games and what is unacceptable in one (the foul in the football game), might well be acceptable in another (Anderson's foul of using McKendrick and tricking the Czech authorities). The essence of sport is compliance with the rules of the game; the essence of utilitarian politics (totalitarianism, ultimately) is that there are no rules other than doing what achieves one's ends. Anderson is quite consistent within this framework; he uses the methods of the opposition in order to overcome them. Despite Anderson's closing remark of the play in Scene 16, 'Ethics is a very complicated business. That's why we have these congresses', the main issues are fundamentally such that a 'child would know the difference'.

What are the 'professional fouls'?

McKendrick in Scene 10 clarifies the point that actions are made within ethical frameworks. As has been already explained, the point at which the action occurs within the framework—or topological form (Scene 8), determines the nature of the ethical act. That is to say, in certain situations, for example, when unethical pressures are very great, in order to maintain the original ethical goal, the action may seemingly become unethical. This more flexible view of ethics is not based on absolute principles (which both McKendrick and Anderson agree do not exist) but on the idea that there are 'a lot of principled people trying to behave as if there were'. This is the basis of Anderson's 'Ethical Fictions' which must have the status of absolute principles. Thus there are two kinds of fouls discernible in the play: those that act entirely against the fiction of the ethical principles and cannot be justified by any catastrophe theory as they do not represent a catastrophic point within the topological form, and those that are justifiable precisely on these terms. And in both these categories, some fouls are of greater importance than others.

The real fouls, or fouls of the former kind, are:

(1) the police planting dollars in Hollar's flat
(2) Broadbent's foul against Deml in the football match.

In the former case, the police behaviour is based on a profound error, as described by Anderson in his lecture in Scene 14, the error of a state seeking to 'impose its values on the very individuals who comprise the State'. In the latter case, Broadbent is acting, analogously with the police, against the fundamental ethics of the game which is not merely for scoring or preventing goals, but for playing skilfully within the rules. Thus his expedient act cannot be justifiable. These two fouls are revealed as being of the same moral order by their proximity in Scene 6.

There are three fouls justifiable on the grounds of the catastrophe theory:

(1) Anderson's lies to the police about the contents of his briefcase
(2) Chetwyn's smuggling out of letters to Amnesty International
(3) the crucial 'foul' of the play, Anderson's planting of Hollar's thesis on McKendrick.

The first of these three is made dubious by Anderson's own stance at the time. Was he not lying more to save himself than to save the thesis? But it could be equally well argued that as a result of his shocking encounter with the police he had already begun to move away from his original and narrower view of ethical behaviour. The second instance, Chetwyn's smuggling, is a direct parallel to Anderson's smuggling of Hollar's thesis and seems to illustrate what would have happened if Anderson had been too scrupulous to use McKendrick. It is very inept to act predictably when dealing with devious and dangerous opponents. The third foul, the planting of the thesis in McKendrick's briefcase and the crowning action of the play, is a complete reversal of Anderson's stance in Scene 3 when he refuses to allow Hollar to plant his thesis in his own luggage: 'You could be getting me into trouble, and your quarrel is not with me. Your action would be unethical on your own terms—one man's dealings with another man'. He does not give McKendrick the ethical choice of choosing whether to be a co-conspirator or not (a skilful reminder of Scene 1). There is some irony in this reversal, as there is irony in McKendrick being the moral mentor of the play and yet an unknowing and unwilling participant in the play's main moral act. But the neatest little ironic touch comes from the police captain's idiomatic mistake in Scene 6: he calls Broadbent's tackle a 'necessary foul'. This is not applicable in a moral sense to Broadbent, but is certainly an apt description of Chetwyn's and Anderson's two fouls.

How are the characters drawn?

Professional Foul is unusual among Stoppard's works in that it contains finer character portrayal than any of his other plays. Stoppard's plays are without exception comedies of ideas, and characterisation has always played a subordinate part. However, Anderson is an outstanding exception.

Anderson

The 'stage' directions at the beginning of this television play give a clear indication of what Anderson is like when we first see him. He is a 'middle-aged, or more' professor from a prestigious university. He 'dabs at his mouth with his napkin', conveying the 'somewhat fastidious impression' called for in the directions. Learned and much travelled, as we hear moments later, he can afford to be detached about the colloquium, indeed to him the colloquium is just an excuse for his hobby—football. He cultivates his detachment with 'wit and paradox. Verbal felicity.' He represents 'A higher civilisation alive and well in the older universities'. These words of McKendrick's in Scene 1 are a summary of what we grow to realise is part of a well-buttressed façade. Because, of course, detachment implies that Anderson needs to distance himself from something. And we are shown a symptom of this need in his anxiety over the 'wagging' wings of the aircraft. Obviously fear is a significant ingredient in the make-up of his character.

We encounter at once the objects of his acts of distancing. First of all it is his younger colleagues McKendrick and Chetwyn, greeted with false enthusiasm and patronage, the main quality of the latter being remoteness, albeit tempered with a little kindness. Secondly, there is Hollar, his former student. He is now in serious trouble and Anderson quite plainly wishes to brush him aside. Only Hollar's persistence forces him to make a small compromise—that of visiting the flat which will involve him in the moral problem of the play. Anderson's weakness is plainly his fear of other people.

This fear has caused him to surround himself with games. On the one hand they are the games of 'ethical fictions' that allow him to function in mental and moral spheres with safe detachment from the real world; on the other hand it is a game itself, football, that provides his emotional involvement and release. His first (there are only two) spontaneous outburst concerns that game in Scene 4, when he gives a passionate description of the Czech team's tactics. This outburst is quite startling, as it follows shortly after Hollar's visit with all its tragic implications, when we saw Anderson maintain a cool detachment.

By Scene 4 we are clearly presented with a fastidious, detached, yet astute and successful man whose passions are channelled into trivial outlets. This is a mixture which while in itself a witty observation of traditional British academics, is not without some potential for development, and it is this development, the gradual overcoming of his inadequacies, that we witness as the play unfolds.

In this respect, Anderson is unique among the characters of the play. He is the only character that has been given the potential for change, and indeed the whole action of the play depends on his growing perception of ethics. All the forces in the play: the philosophical arguments, the sufferings of the Hollars, the actions perpetrated in the name of the Czech state, work upon Anderson and change his attitudes and actions.

In Scene 5 Anderson's statement at the end of Stone's lecture is a succinct refutation of linguistic philosophy. It is also part of the concluding message of the play, that major truths are simple and monolithic. This already provides a criticism, if only for the audience, of his own stance in relation to Hollar in Scene 3. There he obscured the simple truth of Hollar's persecution and his need for help with the rules of a game about manners and contracts. This speech has several functions: while it contributes to the play of ideas, it also reveals Anderson's cleverness, that his vision is actually wider than the rules he sets himself for action. And we also see that he can act well in a crisis, at least when he is on familiar ground.

In Scene 6 the ground is unfamiliar and he is 'out of his depth and afraid'. We see him bluster, and then like St Peter, deny his associations and his better self out of fear. 'I do not know what they are doing here, I do not care what they are doing here'. In his defence of Hollar, when led into conversation with the police captain, he is made to seem unreasonable, but the captain's devious tactics leave their mark. The situation is preposterious as well as dangerous, and obviously Anderson's usual 'rules' cannot encompass it. The nub of the philosophical problem is neatly exposed by the close contrasting of the professional foul of the football match heard on the radio, and the planting of the dollars by the police, the former a matter for 'rules', the latter a matter for 'the fundamental ethic of the individual'. This scene is the first of a series of events that are to work upon Anderson and make him change his mind about the smuggling of Hollar's thesis.

The next event that affects Anderson is McKendrick's definition of morality in Scene 8. Quite unwittingly McKendrick, who is speaking about morality only in general terms, sums up Anderson's first response to Hollar, 'you end up using a moral principle as your excuse for acting against a moral interest. It's a sort of funk'. We then witness Anderson's only other passionate response in the play. The remark has made itself felt. Anderson is made to question his principles. We then see Anderson's prompt response to the sight of Mrs Hollar. The reversal in his attitude has taken place. There is courage and humility in such a change.

In Scene 9 when he meets Mrs Hollar and Sacha, we learn he has made up his mind to take the thesis out of the country, 'He asked me to take it'. Sacha advises him against it, as Anderson is bound to be searched at the airport. We see Anderson's emotional defence-building in his treatment of the boy as an adult, but nevertheless he has become involved enough to apologise for his previous attitudes and to give reassurances and promises of help.

Only in retrospect will the viewer realise that Scene 10 marks the time of Anderson's main actions in defence of Hollar and the 'individual ethic'. He borrows the typewriter to rewrite his lecture, which though originally quite aptly dealing with 'ethical fictions' was obviusly not committed to a support of human rights. He also (though this too is unknown to the viewer) plants the thesis in McKendrick's luggage, a tactic triply justified by the trickery of the Czech police themselves, by Sacha's warning and McKendrick's catastrophe theory. This act is to be justified yet again, by the parallel case of Chetwyn who is caught in the airport with his less cleverly smuggled documents. The next morning, Anderson calmly delivers the lecture in the face of opposition, and equally calmly at the airport in the afternoon faces the customs search. His spasm of anxiety is a joke for the viewer, as the tell-tale bulge in the luggage is the girly magazine, though no doubt his embarrassment is in character and is a formally fitting reference to the start of the play. So too, is his witty composure in the aeroplane when he acquaints McKendrick with the truth. He may have developed his sense of ethical behaviour, but he has not lost his self-command. He leaves Czechoslovakia having learned to act courageously and altruistically, while not allowing these considerations to override his astuteness. He has moved from intellectual detachment to a commitment to human rights. It is a move into the sphere of politics.

McKendrick

It can be argued that, as in Anderson's case, it is the capacity for change that makes a literary character three-dimensional. Though McKendrick's character is as flawed as Anderson's, he remains throughout the play as we first see him: extrovert ('McKendrick's manner is extrovert. Almost breezy'), a straight and enthusiastic thinker in philosophical matters (as his gradually unfolded perception of ethics shows), but a muddled time-server politically ('I sail pretty close to the wind Marx-wise') and in other matters of behaviour, motivated by a crude sensuality ('I wonder if there'll be any decent women'). The quotations all come from Scene 1, and nothing apart from a deepening of the philosophical argument occurs to alter this view of McKendrick. In fact, he very conveniently provides us with an all-round summary of himself at the end of the scene: 'Not a bad life. Science Fiction and sex. And, of course, the philosophical assumptions of social science.'

All Stoppard's characters have a tendency to provide us with convenient summaries, if not of themselves, then of the points of view they are made to represent, or of their, usually wholly accurate, perception of other people. Thus Broadbent is 'an opportunist' in Anderson's view (Scene 2); McKendrick summarises Chetwyn's philosophical stance for us in Scene 1: 'His line is that Aristotle got it more or less right, and St Augustine brought it up to date'; Anderson refutes linguistic philosophy (Scene 5) well before he is ready to act on the refutation, and so on.

It is hard not to draw the conclusion that McKendrick, like so many of Stoppard's characters, is above all a convenience for the action of the play, providing Anderson with his philosophical justifications and the viewer with light relief through the comic contradictions he embodies. Apart from that, he takes his shape from broadly drawn traits that are recognisable as typical of many present-day university lecturers. Of these, his left-wing political sympathies and attendant interest in popular culture are most typical. But the portrayal is saved from mere caricature by precise qualifications: with the political adherence comes a sense of social inferiority (Doctor, 'only of philosophy') which leads to excessive class-consciousness and ultimately snobbery, though to be fair, in McKendrick's case it never seems to go further than passive envy of Anderson's position ('A higher civilisation' and 'one of life's cricketers'). He is thus full of contradictions: left-wing but socially aspiring, a clever philosopher but a vulgar hedonist, moralistic but totally unable to put his thoughts into practice ('I wouldn't do it. Would you?'—Scene 16). Therein lies much of the humour and irony of the play. Still, his enthusiasm for philosphy that realistically and consistently allows him to help guide Anderson on to the best path of action, gives him a warmth and a significant presence that makes him memorable. He provides an interesting contrast to the careful Anderson.

Sacha

The portrayal of Sacha also allows one to think that ideas override character in Stoppard's plays. Here is a boy who is abnormally developed for his age in terms of his linguistic abilities and responsibilities. But a small boy is required to illustrate the point about the simplicity of human rights, as well as to emphasise the terror and pathos of the situation. He is a useful instrument in showing Anderson's limited emotional sphere; he cannot be at ease with Sacha as a child and cannot cope with his tears. But Sacha's credibility is perhaps saved by the reflection that some children grow old before their time in conditions where adult members of the family are under severe pressure.

Stoppard seems to prefer, apart from Anderson, the static character who best contributes to the play of ideas in his drama. However, Stoppard's humorous approach allows him to give life to his characters by means of social observations that border on satire. The characters can embody pertinent comments about social milieux. We see in *Professional Foul* a cross-section of Anglo-saxon philosophical academe represented by Anderson, McKendrick, Chetwyn and Stone, each with a character to match his brand of philosophy. Less significantly, but nevertheless amusingly, a couple of sly comments are made about journalists, their dress and their language. Equivalent satirical commentary is found in his stage works.

Part 4

Hints for study

A play presents the reader with particular difficulties. It is not just a question of imagining the work as a real event, but of imagining it as a *performance*, and in this case, a television performance. You should read the 'stage' directions carefully and imagine the visual impact of each setting. In television drama especially, it is quite possible that the mere sight of something is of dramatic significance, like the briefcase in *Professional Foul*. Each change of scene will contribute to the rhythm of the play and telling points can be made through contrasting scenes. In *Professional Foul* the comfortable world of the international jet, hotel and lavishly equipped colloquium hall contrasts sharply with the squalid flat of the Hollars and emphasises the private trauma of the Western professor's encounter with the realities of life in the Soviet bloc.

This play also shows clearly that it is sometimes to no purpose to think too much in terms of character and realistic motives. Dramatic characters can be, and not just in Stoppard, symbols for ideas or embodiments of generalisations about significant types.

Every effort should be made to see or create a performance of the play. Even reading the script aloud with others will highlight significant aspects that could easily be lost in a solitary reading. 'Drama' originally meant activity and its true flavour can only be experienced through participation.

All writing worthy of the name literature repays close study. Words should not be taken at their face value; usually they have a significance beyond their immediate meaning and mostly this significance is carefully calculated by the writer. You should not be afraid of ambiguities if they arise; there is not always an answer to the questions posed in works of art. It can even happen that the complexities of a work of art seemingly take on a life of their own so that the work finally means more than the writer originally intended. *Hamlet* might be considered an example of this.

Professional Foul however, is too controlled and economical a piece to fall into this category. Almost every utterance and every character contributes to the action, the drama, which is, most appropriately, an examination of the principles upon which real action should be based. Many questions are raised but no *direct* answer is given. It is clearly *suggested* through the final action of Anderson, and the suggestion is more definite and committed (to Western liberal ideals) than in any of Stoppard's previous works.

In reading the play you might find it helpful to bear a musical analogy in mind: in each line there are many things going on at once; two or three themes can be played at one time and still the whole harmonises and is pleasing and comprehensible. Literary complexities function much like counterpoint in music. Look for these simultaneous themes; make a note of them when they occur in the text and trace them all through the play. In *Professional Foul* trace separately the development of the action, the characters, the philosophical ideas, the humour and the politics, and then when you are sure you have a clear idea of them all, consider how they are related to one another and make up the dramatic whole.

Lastly there is the consideration of essay writing techniques and examination techniques. You should not be reading these Notes now unless you have already read the play *several* times. Once for an idea of the action or 'story', a second time for develoment of character, a third time for the philosophy, fourth time for humour and politics, and each time you should be making notes. *Then* you are ready to consider other people's opinions about it and to write about it. *Bad essays are almost invariably caused by lack of preparation. There are no short-cuts*, though concentrating and being methodical save time and yield better results.

If you have a choice, choose a question which interests you. An answer that conveys genuine interest in the subject is always attractive to the reader or examiner. Always stick to the question; do not write down everything you know about the play. Always make notes first and organise your notes into a clear argument before you write. This is time well spent in an examination. The very act of note-making and organising clarifies your thoughts and develops coherent arguments in your mind.

Try to find suitable quotations to illustrate your main points. It shows close acquaintance with the work, and this is what the examiner is looking for. It also keeps your arguments strictly to the evidence of the text and again, examiners look for this approach. So a wise student finds significant passages in his set works and learns them before the examination. The quotations may be very short, but should illustrate a significant aspect of the work discussed. Some quotations of this type are given below:

Scene 1: 'Have you noticed the way the wings keep *wagging*?'
    'His line is that Aristotle got it more or less right, and St Augustine brought it up to date.'
    'There are some rather dubious things happening in Czechoslovakia. Ethically.'

'Ethical Fictions as Ethical Foundations.'

Scene 2: 'He's an opportunist more than anything.'

Scene 3: 'The ethics of the State must be judged against the fundamental ethics of the individual.'

'I observe my son for example.'

Scene 5: 'the important truths are simple and monolithic.'

Scene 6: '—a necessary foul.'

Scene 8: 'There's a point—the catastrophic point—where your progress along one line of behaviour jumps you into the opposite line; the principle reverses itself at the point where a rational man would abandon it.'

'So you end up using a moral principle as your excuse for acting against a moral interest. It's a sort of funk—'

Scene 9: 'He asked me to take it.'

Scene 14: 'a child would know the difference.'

'There is a sense of right and wrong which precedes utterance. It is individually experienced and it concerns one person's dealings with another person. From this experience we have built a system ... of recognition of individual right.'

Scene 16: 'I wouldn't do it. Would you?'

'No. He should have known he'd be searched.'

'I'm afraid I reversed a principle.'

'It's not quite playing the game is it?'

'Ethics is a very complicated business. That's why they have these congresses.'

When you have jotted down your ideas in note form, arrange them into a sequence of paragraphs, cut out repetitions and check that there is a logical development in your arguments. This is the most important and time-consuming stage of the planning. Choose apt quotations to prove your major points.

When you start writing, make sure each of your paragraphs starts with a clear statement of the paragraph topic so that your essay does not degenerate into a long list of directionless information about the play. When you reach the end of your arguments, *sum up* your essay in a concluding paragraph. This should draw together your preceding arguments and should not introduce any major new idea.

Here are three sample essays on three major aspects of the play. They are just over a thousand words in length, the average for examination essays written in less than an hour.

1. 'Stoppard has written a script much of which could have been produced by any competent screenwriter' (Ronald Hayman). Do you think this is a just view of *Professional Foul*?

Plan for Essay 1
(1) Compare competent screen-writer and expectations of Stoppard
  (a) television drama
  (b) Stoppard's stage works
  (c) how *Professional Foul* compares; its political purpose and multiple themes
  (d) outline of complexities of the play
(2) Characterisation
(3) Philosophical issues and parable of football match
(4) Social commentary and satire
(5) Roots of critic's disappointment
  (a) complexities obscured by realism
  (b) Stoppard's reputation from his stage works
(6) Conclusion: the smooth blend of the play's several parts

The quotation implies that the general standard of television script-writing is somehow lower in quality than what we usually expect from the pen of Tom Stoppard. It would be fair to say that much of television drama is simple in form, that is, linear in action, and that the drama, as often as not, centres on the action itself, holding the audience through twists and turns of a suspenseful plot. The emphasis is on a good story. Stoppard's earlier stage works have led us to expect something far more complex than this. *Jumpers* and *Travesties* rely on a play of ideas, on elaborate pastiche, innovations in form and unexpected visual humour more than on simple narrative. The mixture is described by Stoppard, a little pejoratively, as 'seriousness compromised by frivolity'. *Professional Foul* does seem to break away from these complexities, and the action of the play could be regarded as a simple anecdote. There is reason to believe that this is quite deliberate on Stoppard's part. He has observed that there is 'a sort of code' for the writing of television plays, a code that enables the audience to identify easily with the characters. He is tempering his style to suit the accepted norms of the medium. It should also be borne in mind that the play was written to mark Prisoner of Conscience Year (1977) and its form reflects both witnesses' accounts in Amnesty International evidence files and Stoppard's interest in communicating the plight of these prisoners clearly and simply to a large audience. However, the play offers a great deal more than a clear and suspenseful presentation of an Amnesty International report. The critic has been misled by an apparent simplicity: the play encompasses many themes underpinning the main action.

In the first scene we encounter the two main characters, Anderson and McKendrick. They are typically Stoppardian in that they represent certain ideas and certain social types. However, unusually for Stoppard, Anderson is also a portrayal of a man undergoing a moral change. What these two represent is put across with an economy and realism that almost amount to cunning. Each sentence of the first scene contributes to a revelation of their characters, their philosophical stances and, moreover, to an outline of the whole setting of the play. McKendrick has a useful knack of summing up characters, including his own: 'Not a bad life. Science Fiction and sex. And, of course, the philosophical assumptions of social science.' Seemingly realistic trivia actually reveal significant qualities or limitations of character, such as Anderson's anxiety, which are part of the whole action of the play: 'Have you noticed the way the wings keep *wagging*?'

The same economy and realism of style are used in conveying the philosophical argument of the play. The spectators of the play are invited to participate in the gradual revelation of the moral issues through the stances of the various characters. Thus McKendrick provides the most sophisticated and also the most workable of the moral solutions with his catastrophe theory while Chetwyn is too naively straightforward with his Aristotelian deism, and Stone, the Quinian linguistic philosopher, can offer little of practical value. We are invited to learn of these theories and to develop our moral view through the character of Anderson whose own original stance, a structure of rules or 'ethical fictions', is found to be sadly wanting in the face of the Czech state's persecution of Hollar. The debate is supported by a parable of a 'professional foul' committed in a football match (Anderson's real reason for coming to Czechoslovakia), so that there is even an opportunity for the audience to grasp the complexities on a simpler and more emotional plane should the philosophy prove too abstruse. They are invited to make a revealing comparison between Broadbent's foul in the match and Anderson's foul against McKendrick. They are left to draw their own conclusions after having been shown the issues with great concision on various levels: intellectually through philosophical debate, visually and emotionally through the metaphor of the football match and the encounter with the Hollar family.

The complexities of the play do not stop with these ethical arguments. There is also social commentary and mild satire of academe in the presentation of the philosophers. McKendrick is excessively class-conscious ('Dr McKendrick.' 'Only of philosophy.') and is an ironic portrayal of a university Marxist. Anderson on the other hand represents 'A higher civilization alive and well in the older universities'. Journalists do not escape Stoppard's wit. Their attire is likened to Eastern European plain-clothes policemen and their style is mimicked with relish: 'There'll be Czechs bouncing in the streets of Prague tonight as bankruptcy stares English football in the face.' There is much witty and elegant humour in these portrayals skilfully tempered to remain within the bounds of realism, while Ronald Hayman, in this quotation, seems to be yearning for the extravagances of Stoppard's stage works.

Hayman's disappointment may be based, first, on Stoppard's realism which has stood in the way of his comprehension of the play's complex philosophical arguments. It could be argued that these arguments do not become clear in one viewing and that some aspects are better appreciated in a reading, or at least after several viewings. However, the same is also true of the stage works of Chekhov, Ibsen, and so on. Secondly, Hayman may be disappointed because, although Stoppard has gained a reputation for audacity in the theatre, there is no doubt that he has been consistently conservative in the form of his television plays. There is little exploitation of the flexibility of that medium, but on the other hand, he uses to the full its capacity to involve the audience closely in a realistic situation.

It must be concluded that the play is one that invites a moral commitment, a commitment to the idea of individual human rights. As such it has a didactic purpose for which television is well suited because of its capacity to involve its large audience intimately in a situation. Stoppard takes hold of the audience by using the popular method of suspense, presents it with characters that are recognisable and made sympathetic through humorously presented weaknesses and adds to these easily digested ingredients a sophisticated moral argument that can be comprehended emotionally as well as intellectually. He sets out to involve and convert a wide-ranging audience to the support of human rights, while entertaining and amusing them as well. It is a clever mixture, and so smoothly blended that it is all too easy to lose sight of its varied parts. This is perhaps the root of Hayman's disappointment; it is Stoppard's very competence that has camouflaged his deeper purpose and made one rather superficial critic see him as just another television script-writer.

---

2. 'Ethics is a very complicated business.' How relevant is Anderson's comment to the understanding of *Professional Foul*?'

Plan for Essay 2
(1) Role of ethics in the play
   (a) morality of Anderson's action
   (b) human rights
   (c) play's action depends on beliefs of protagonists
(2) How complex are the ethics?

(a) complex enough to warrant an 'off-stage' colloquium
(b) Anderson is the assessor of each belief
(3) Real drama lies in Anderson's understanding of the ethics and his change of attitude
(4) Outline of philosophical stances presented in the play; McKendrick and the sight of the injustices as the mentors of the action
(5) Ethical complications of Anderson's actions
   (a) lecture
   (b) the planting of the thesis
   (c) the comparison of the football foul
   (d) McKendrick's unwitting clarification
(6) Conclusion: Anderson's comment apt, but also symptomatic of Stoppard's lightness of touch

To answer the question, it is best to consider the role of ethics in the play. There can be no doubt that the play presents the means whereby we can judge the morality of Anderson's action in planting Hollar's thesis in McKendrick's briefcase, while also rehearsing the arguments for human rights. The play is about ethics. The action of the play depends on the beliefs of the protagonists, of which one is the Czech state. In this respect, it is a wholly Stoppardian play, where the witty presentation of philosophical ideas is always the central drama.

In the course of the play's arguments on the question of human rights, we learn that the issue is not complicated as 'a child would know the difference' between its rights and wrongs. Yet the presence of the philosophers shows us that the issue has been so obscured that a major effort of clarification is required. It is of course deliberately apposite that the play is set around a philosophical congress, but the main philosophical debate is 'off-stage'. Each protagonist, including the Czech state, presents his point of view, almost at cross-purposes, apropos of nothing (rather like the trivial conversations which open Scene 8 in the hotel dining room), and in ignorance of Anderson's growing awareness of his own moral inadequacy. Each protagonist's testimony works upon Anderson whose wit and discrimination (his capacity for 'paradox') enable him to make a moral commitment so that he skilfully arranges for the persecuted Hollar's thesis to be smuggled out of the country.

Thus the real drama lies in Anderson's understanding of the ethical stance of each protagonist and its effect upon him. And herein lies a great part of the complications. The fact that the story of the progress of the thesis is made dominant by the tricks of suspense introduced by Stoppard, should not obscure the drama of Anderson's change. Nor should Stoppard's lightness of touch on the philosophical issues, perhaps based on an over-optimistic assumption that a significant proportion of his audience will understand them from the brief references made in passing, obscure their central importance. The crucial nature of the philosophical questions is underlined by the parable of the football match, where a 'professional foul' of another order is committed for the sake of moral clarification through comparison.

The colloquium allows Stoppard a realistic excuse for a presentation of current philosophical thought in Britain. McKendrick represents 'applied philosophy' with his catastrophic theory; Chetwyn a new fashion for old-fashioned Aristotelianism plus deism, Stone represents Quinian linguistic philosophy, and Anderson an eclectic mainstream. The dynamism of the situation is supplied by Anderson's character flaw: he is initially unable to commit himself to moral action, but is prevailed upon to change his stance in part by McKendrick's moral argument and in part by witnessing the injust treatment and sufferings of the Hollars. He is thus finally able to make and act out a commitment to the support of human rights.

The remaining part of the ethical complications lies in the nature of Anderson's actions. On the one hand the philosophical argument reaches its climax in Anderson's rewritten lecture of Scenes 11 and 14 where he manages to outline the case for human rights before he is 'foully' interrupted by the censorship of the Czech state. His argument is not without difficulties since it ultimately rests upon the defence of what is virtually a human instinct, the notion of justice that even a child recognises. But the play focuses more attention upon Anderson's action, the planting of Hollar's thesis in McKendrick's luggage. This is a parallel to the 'professional foul' of the football match, though the parallel is to some extent obscured by the different sphere of its action. McKendrick clarifies the issues at stake in his drunken speeches of Scene 10. 'Now, listen to me', he says, 'I'm a professional philosopher. You'll do well to listen to what I have to say.' And thus alerted, we hear that it is a question of 'the whole *ethos*'. The whole point of football is skilful play within certain rules, whereas that condition, the constriction of rules, hardly applies to the question of human rights, particularly when it arises in a situation where there are no rules other than expediency: Anderson himself witnessed the framing of Hollar by the police planting dollars in his flat. In such circumstances ordinary rules of fair play cannot work. Chetwyn illustrates this; he is caught taking out letters to Amnesty International. McKendrick again provides the philosophical justification for Anderson's 'particular act of expediency' in Scene 8, indeed his opinion awakens Anderson to the situation. 'There's a point—the catastrophe point—where your progress along one line of behaviour jumps you into the opposite line; the principle reverses itself at the point where a rational man would abandon it.' Thus a moral principle may have to be abandoned in order to uphold a moral interest. So Anderson deceives his colleague and takes a minor risk at the latter's expense in order to support human rights.

Anderson's closing comments are apt. But they are also symptomatic of Stoppard's style. Anderson lightly allows McKendrick the benefit of the doubt, as he can well afford to. Though the play is didactic, it is not obviously so; the viewer is in much the same position as Anderson; the arguments are free to work upon our minds. There are strong pointers, of which McKendrick's blustering inaction is one, and it would be hard to conclude that his angry protestations in the final scene are valid. But we are left to decide this for ourselves. Stoppard would no more force the issue than would Anderson himself. The debate resounds in our minds as we reach to turn off the television. The debate will continue—'That's why they have these congresses'.

---

3. 'Characterisation is not in itself one of Stoppard's strong points.' Consider this comment in relation to *Professional Foul*.

Plan for Essay 3
(1) (a) Clear the ground: Stoppard's previous works; plays of ideas not of relationships
(b) But interested in satire and pastiche. Interested in surface impressions. Interested in humour
(c) His plays represent a progression. Characterisation progressive
(2) *Professional Foul*
(a) Each philosopher represents a philosophical stance. The other characters indispensable to the action; no one there for the sake of character interest
(b) Anderson is the major exception:
his philosophical stance
his eclecticism
his forced involvement
his progress from detachment to moral and political commitment
(c) McKendrick also an exception.
Satirical portrayal of left-wing university lecturer
Good philosopher but poor man of action
Embodies many contradictions, therefore humorous
Finally sympathetic character. Sum greater than parts
(d) Embryonic form of Chetwyn
(3) Conclusion
(a) *Professional Foul* takes Stoppard's characterisation further
(b) Role of television
(c) Stoppard is playwright of ideas, not of psychological drama

Stoppard's previous stage works, including his theatrical farces, are plays of ideas and not plays of relationships and character development.

Rosencrantz and Guildenstern are Dead (1966) is not a play about the two characters of the title, but is a play about the terror of existence. *Jumpers* (1972) and *Travesties* (1974) continue a development of his philosophical ideas. The arguments of these plays become more closely involved with specific and contemporary issues and lead ultimately to the topicality and practicality of *Professional Foul* (1977). Throughout his plays, Stoppard lightens the drama with elaborate wit, and with satire and pastiche, so that he *is* interested in surface impressions of characters and in the humorous contradictions which they embody. As the debate of ideas in his plays comes closer to a clear commitment to Western liberalism, so the characters who are the explorers and catalysts of these ideas become more detailed and more differentiated in their portrayal. There is quite a progression from the near-similarity and near-anonymity of Rosencrantz and Guildenstern to the portrayal of George Moore in *Jumpers* and of Carr and Lenin in *Travesties*.

In *Professional Foul*, each of the four philosophers represents a philosophical stance, and together they present a cross-section of the current philosophical academe. As such they are mouthpieces, and one of them, Stone, serves no purpose beyond that. The other characters, the Hollars, the policemen, and not least the English journalists, are indispensable to the action and possess very little to make them recognisable individuals. They are a sum of their functions (police captain), or a means of conveying clever pastiche (Grayson). None of them is there for the sheer interest of his character. This is an observation which it would not be possible to make about an Ibsen or Chekhov play. However, there is at least one major exception to this state of affairs: Anderson.

As far as Anderson's philosophical interests are concerned, they are significantly eclectic. He represents the mainstream of British philosophy; he is a close relative of George Moore in *Jumpers*. But Anderson's eclecticism goes beyond his immediate academic interests. He is eclectic in his assessment of the various philosophical points of view represented at the colloquium, and is equally discriminating in his judgement of the morality of Czech society when he is forced to witness it at close hand.

When we are first presented with Anderson, we are subtly shown that he is an isolated and self-satisfied figure, anxious indeed not to be involved with others. He is frightened of the modern world ('I wouldn't be nervous about flying if the wings didn't wag'), detached from his fellow philosophers (his stock remark, 'excellent university'), and immune to the problems of others ('You could be getting me into trouble'). However, fate decrees, or Hollar decrees, that he should become involved and from the confrontation with the police at

Hollar's flat, we witness the gradual piercing of his emotional and moral armour and by Scene 9 a complete reversal of his attitude.

While the sight of the Hollar's plight and his frustrated anger at the police corruption play a part in his conversion—'Mrs Hollar—I will do everything I can for him', a second major influence on him is the philo-sophising of McKendrick, another outstanding character in the play, and indeed in Stoppard's work as a whole.

McKendrick, unlike Anderson, is a static character and we learn of all the chief aspects to his personality by the end of Scene 1. 'Not a bad life. Science Fiction and sex. And, of course, the philosphical assump-tions of social science.' But he is drawn in the round, so to speak. Though there is no moral development in him, he looms large in the play with his blustering enthusiasm for his subject and plentiful philo-sophical advice, which proves to be sound. Indeed, his interpretation of the catastrophe theory provides Anderson with the solution to the problem of getting Hollar's thesis out of the country. His major flaw is his inability to put his sound theories into action. 'I wouldn't do it. Would you?' His minor flaws provide most of the humour of the play, for he is the embodiment of the slack moral contradictions of British academe, left-wing but snobbish (see the drunken scene with football-ers), a clever philosopher but a vulgar hedonist (writes for porno-graphic magazines), a moraliser but unable to grace his thoughts with matching deeds. Yet he becomes greater than the sum of his parts. Maybe it is the generosity with which he dispenses his ideas; he is made memorable through his enthusiasm. He himself learns little from the weekend in Prague, but Anderson and we, the audience, learn much from him.

Chetwyn, though shadowy, begins to grow larger than his philo-sohical views in his rashness to help the Czechs. True, his failure to smuggle out the letters to Amnesty International proves the expediency of Anderson's action and helps to make it seem more acceptable morally, and in this he is simply a dramatic device in the play. Never-theless, the few aspects of his persona that Stoppard indicates, are cleverly observed and logically consistent character traits, so that he very nearly becomes a recognisable individual.

Stoppard has taken the portrayal of characters a good deal further in *Professional Foul* than ever before in his plays. This could be seen as part of a process of his own development: as his philosophical games and ideas link up more with real issues so the characters that convey them become more realistic as well. Stoppard is also on record as say-ing that television drama demands greater characterisation and that television audiences require to be able to identify with the protagonists; this too could be a reason for the outstanding characterisations in this play. However, we should not allow ourselves to be too conditioned by the great tradition of the psychological dramas dating back to the late nineteenth century; plays of ideas with their greater scope for humour and satire are also a valid form of theatre, and it is primarily to this form that Stoppard's plays belong.

Some further questions

1. Compare and contrast the characters of McKendrick and Anderson.
2. Describe the develoment of Anderson's character in the play.
3. 'The characters of *Professional Foul* are mere mouthpieces of Stoppard's philosophical arguments. They can scarcely be said to possess individual personality.' Do you agree?
4. What are the philosophical arguments underlying *Professional Foul*?
5. 'Stoppard makes his points altogether too subtly in *Professional Foul* so that the viewer can follow little more than the main action.' Discuss.
6. '*Professional Foul* is a play to be read rather than seen.' Discuss.
7. '*Professional Foul* confirms Stoppard as a clever but bloodless playwright.' Is this so?
8. Show how Stoppard uses the play *Professional Foul* to examine the principles upon which practice is, or should be, based.
9. *Professional Foul* is a foray into 'committed art'. Discuss.
10. 'Politically committed though *Professional Foul* is, it is little more than an anecdote.' Do you agree?
11. Do you think *Professional Foul* will stand the test of time? Support your answer by detailed references to the text.
12. Does humour have a role in *Professional Foul*, and if so, how is it created?
13. Discuss how Stoppard achieves his effects by analysing Scene 8 (*Interior. Hotel dining room*).
14. Wherein lies the drama of *Professional Foul*?
15. Why is the play *Professional Foul* so named?
16. 'Economy is the hallmark of Stoppard's style in *Professional Foul*.' Do you agree?

Part 5

Suggestions for further reading

The text

Professional Foul in *Every Good Boy Deserves Favour (A Play for Actors and Orchestra) and Professional Foul (A Play for Television)*, Faber and Faber, London, 1978. Reprinted 1978 and 1979. (*Professional Foul* was first shown on BBC TV in September 1977; *Every Good Boy Deserves Favour* was first performed at the Festival Hall, London in July 1977.)

Other works by Tom Stoppard

A Walk on the Water (on television, 1963; produced in Hamburg, 1964; revised as *The Preservation of George Riley*, on television, 1964; revised as *Enter a Free Man*, produced in London, 1968), Faber and Faber, London, 1968.

The Gamblers (produced in Bristol, 1965). Unpublished.

Tango, adapted from a play by Sławomir Mrożek, translated by Nicholas Bethell (produced in London, 1966), Cape, London, 1968.

A Separate Peace (on television, 1966). Published in *Playbill 2*, edited by Alan Durband, Hutchinson, London, 1969.

Rosencrantz and Guildenstern are Dead (produced in Edinburgh, 1966; revised version produced in London at the National Theatre, 1967), Faber and Faber, London, 1967.

The Real Inspector Hound (produced in London, 1968), Faber and Faber, London, 1968.

Albert's Bridge and If You're Glad I'll be Frank: Two Plays for Radio (*Albert's Bridge*, BBC broadcast, 1967, produced in New York, 1975; *If You're Glad*, BBC broadcast, 1965), Faber and Faber, London, 1969.

After Magritte (produced in London, Ambiance Theatre, 1970), Faber and Faber, London, 1971.

Dogg's Our Pet (produced in London, Ambiance Theatre, 1971), in *Six of the Best*, Inter-Action Imprint, London, 1976.

Jumpers (produced in London, National Theatre, 1972), Faber and Faber, London, 1972.

The House of Bernarda Alba, adaption of the play by F. Garcia Lorca (produced in London, 1973). Unpublished.

Artist Descending a Staircase and Where Are They Now? Two Plays for Radio (Artist Descending, BBC broadcast, 1972; *Where Are They Now?,* BBC broadcast, 1970), Faber and Faber, London, 1973.

Travesties (produced in London, Aldwych, 1974), Faber and Faber, London, 1975.

Dirty Linen, and New-Found-Land (produced in London, Ambiance Theatre, 1976), Faber and Faber, London, 1976.

Night and Day (produced in London, Phoenix Theatre, 1978), Faber and Faber, London, 1978.

Dogg's Hamlet and Cahoot's Macbeth (produced in London, Collegiate Theatre, 1979), Faber and Faber, London, 1980.

Undiscovered Country (a version of Arthur Schnitzler's *Das weite Land*) (produced in London, National Theatre, 1979), Faber and Faber, London, 1980.

On the Razzle (produced in London, National Theatre, 1981), Faber and Faber, London, 1981.

The Real Thing (produced in London, 1982), Faber and Faber, London, 1982.

Screenplays by Tom Stoppard

The Engagement (1969)
The Romantic Englishwoman (with T. Wiseman, 1975)
Despair (1978)
The Human Factor (1979)

Other radio plays by Tom Stoppard

The Dissolution of Dominic Boot (BBC broadcast, 1964)
M is for Moon among Other Things (BBC broadcast, 1964)

Other television plays

This Way Out with Samuel Boot (1964), unperformed
Teeth (1967)
Another Moon Called Earth (1967)
Neutral Ground (1968)
One Pair of Eyes (documentary, 1972)
Boundaries (with Clive Exton, 1975)
Three Men in a Boat
    (from the novel by Jerome K. Jerome, 1975)

Novel

Lord Malquist and Mr Moon, Blond, London, 1966 (later editions by Faber and Faber).

Short stories

Introduction 2 (with others), Faber and Faber, London, 1964.

Criticism and background reading

ABRAMS, M.H.: *A Glossary of Literary Terms*, Holt Rinehart and Winston, New York, 1971 (3rd edition). A clear, concise account of the major terms used in literary criticism. Alphabetically arranged. It is essential for a student of literature to have a reference book of this type, and for its size the Abrams *Glossary* is good.

BIGSBY, C.W.E.: *Tom Stoppard*, Longman, Harlow, 1976. A perceptive and thorough thirty-page pamphlet published for the British Council. Background reading only, as its date precludes any mention of *Professional Foul*. Gives one of the best bibliographies of critical studies up to 1976. Obscures the essential issue of Stoppard's foreign origins somewhat, but the commissioning body for the pamphlet may be the reason for that.

BIGSBY, C.W.E. (ED.): *Contemporary English Drama*, Edward Arnold, London, 1981. A collection of essays by various critics on some contemporary playwrights and aspects of their backgrounds. Contains an essay on Stoppard by Ruby Cohn, in the last analysis hostile in attitude and hence, for the inexperienced student, dangerously dismissive. The book is more useful for its other essays: on the Royal Court Theatre for example, as well as on Osborne, Pinter and theatrical language, and so on.

BUHR, RICHARD J.: 'Epistemology and Ethics in Tom Stoppard's *Professional Foul*' in *Comparative Drama*, Kalamazoo, Mich., Vol. 13, pp.320–29, 1979. This gives the philosophical background to *Professional Foul*, and analyses the dilemma Anderson faces between his own ethical rules and human rights. It concludes that Anderson attains 'a certain heroic stature' in finding the courage to break his ethical rules when he discovers that they support the suffering and falsehoods that he encounters in Prague.

HAYMAN, RONALD: *Tom Stoppard*, Contemporary Playwrights Series, 3rd edition, Heinemann, London, 1979. This contains two interviews with Stoppard and brief analyses of nearly all of his works, including five paragraphs on *Professional Foul*. It is really a collection of short individual introductions to his works, containing no general view except what Stoppard himself says in the interviews. Bitty, but clear.

NIGHTINGALE, BENEDICT: *An Introduction to Fifty Modern British Plays*, Pan Books, London, 1982. One critic's virtuoso account of his fifty favourite British plays from Barrie's *The Admirable Crichton* (1902) to Trevor Griffiths's *Comedians* (1975). It includes a general essay on Stoppard as well as analytical accounts of *Rosencrantz and Guildenstern are Dead* and *Jumpers*. Good background reading, and gives a brief placing of *Professional Foul* in the general scheme of Stoppard's work.

SALGADO, GAMINI: *English Drama, A Critical Introduction*, Edward Arnold, London, 1980. A critical survey of English drama from the Middle Ages to the present day; refined in its judgements and a joy to read as criticism. Background reading for a wider study of the British theatre, as only two pages are specifically on Stoppard. But in that short space, Salgado rightly emphasises that Stoppard's strength lies in the lightness of his touch and in his theatrical parodies, sources of misunderstanding for his more ham-fisted critics.

TAYLOR, J.R.: *Anger and After*, Methuen, London, 1962, and Penguin Books, Harmondsworth, 1963. A useful exposition, for the student studying Stoppard in a wider context, of the post-World War II British theatre. There is little information specifically on Stoppard, but the book gives a very detailed account of the new wave of energy which hit the British theatre in the late fifties and which swept Stoppard among others into a career of dramatic writing.

TYNAN, KENNETH: *Show People*, Weidenfeld and Nicolson, London, 1980. A motley collection of essays on show business people. The eighty-page account of Tom Stoppard, though anecdotal, contains much that is of interest to the student of *Professional Foul*. It describes Stoppard's increasing involvement with dissidents in Czechoslovakia, especially with the writer Vaclav Havel.

STOPPARD, TOM: 'Something to Declare', *Sunday Times*, London, 25 February, 1968. An article on the principles behind Stoppard's writing, which summarises in his own words his stance before his more recent forages into moral/political commitment. It contains the much quoted 'I burn with no causes. I cannot say that I write with any social objective'.

STOPPARD, TOM: 'Ambushes for the Audience: Towards a High Comedy of Ideas' (interview with the Editors of *Theatre Quarterly*), *Theatre Quarterly*, Vol. IV, No. 14, May–July 1974. Revealing interview about Stoppard's childhood, youth and beginnings as a writer, a personal account of his first successes and of the dialectical philosophy of detachment that his early work embodies. Stoppard goes on to give a reasoned account of his rejection of totalitarianism, of much interest to the student of *Professional Foul*. Contains his own aphoristic summary of himself as a playwright: 'seriousness compromised by frivolity'. One of the main sources for Part I of these Notes.

WHITAKER, THOMAS R.: *Tom Stoppard*, Macmillan Modern Dramatists series, Macmillan, London, 1983. The most complete and up-to-date account of Stoppard's writings currently available. More scholarly than penetrating. Contains very little on *Professional Foul*. Recommended as background reading for students studying Stoppard's works as a whole. Good American-centred critical bibliography.

The author of these notes

BENEDIKTE UTTENTHAL was educated at the University of Cambridge where she read English, and at the University of Essex where she took a postgraduate degree in Comparative Literature. She spent five years (1972–7) working in the Arts Faculty of the Open University, during two years of which she was a contributing member of the Drama Course Team. Since then she has worked widely in the fields of Further and Adult Education, and has lectured part-time for Stirling University in their department of English Studies. In 1982 she was appointed Education Officer in one of Scotland's penal institutions.

York Notes: list of titles

CHINUA ACHEBE
A Man of the People
Arrow of God
Things Fall Apart

EDWARD ALBEE
Who's Afraid of Virginia Woolf?

ELECHI AMADI
The Concubine

ANONYMOUS
Beowulf
Everyman

AYI KWEI ARMAH
The Beautyful Ones Are Not Yet Born

W. H. AUDEN
Selected Poems

JANE AUSTEN
Emma
Mansfield Park
Northanger Abbey
Persuasion
Pride and Prejudice
Sense and Sensibility

HONORÉ DE BALZAC
Le Père Goriot

SAMUEL BECKETT
Waiting for Godot

SAUL BELLOW
Henderson, The Rain King

ARNOLD BENNETT
Anna of the Five Towns
The Card

WILLIAM BLAKE
Songs of Innocence, Songs of Experience

ROBERT BOLT
A Man For All Seasons

HAROLD BRIGHOUSE
Hobson's Choice

ANNE BRONTË
The Tenant of Wildfell Hall

CHARLOTTE BRONTË
Jane Eyre

EMILY BRONTË
Wuthering Heights

ROBERT BROWNING
Men and Women

JOHN BUCHAN
The Thirty-Nine Steps

JOHN BUNYAN
The Pilgrim's Progress

BYRON
Selected Poems

ALBERT CAMUS
L'Etranger (The Outsider)

GEOFFREY CHAUCER
Prologue to the Canterbury Tales
The Clerk's Tale
The Franklin's Tale
The Knight's Tale
The Merchant's Tale
The Miller's Tale
The Nun's Priest's Tale
The Pardoner's Tale
The Wife of Bath's Tale
Troilus and Criseyde

ANTON CHEKOV
The Cherry Orchard

SAMUEL TAYLOR COLERIDGE
Selected Poems

WILKIE COLLINS
The Moonstone

SIR ARTHUR CONAN DOYLE
The Hound of the Baskervilles

WILLIAM CONGREVE
The Way of the World

JOSEPH CONRAD
Heart of Darkness
Lord Jim
Nostromo
The Secret Agent
Victory
Youth and *Typhoon*

STEPHEN CRANE
The Red Badge of Courage

BRUCE DAWE
Selected Poems

WALTER DE LA MARE
Selected Poems

DANIEL DEFOE
A Journal of the Plague Year
Moll Flanders
Robinson Crusoe

CHARLES DICKENS
A Tale of Two Cities
Bleak House
David Copperfield
Dombey and Son
Great Expectations
Hard Times
Little Dorrit
Oliver Twist
Our Mutual Friend
The Pickwick Papers

EMILY DICKINSON
Selected Poems

JOHN DONNE
Selected Poems

JOHN DRYDEN
Selected Poems

GERALD DURRELL
My Family and Other Animals

GEORGE ELIOT
Adam Bede
Middlemarch
Silas Marner
The Mill on the Floss

T. S. ELIOT
Four Quartets
Murder in the Cathedral
Selected Poems
The Cocktail Party
The Waste Land

J. G. FARRELL
The Siege of Krishnapur

GEORGE FARQUHAR
The Beaux Stratagem

WILLIAM FAULKNER
Absalom, Absalom!
The Sound and the Fury

HENRY FIELDING
Joseph Andrews
Tom Jones

F. SCOTT FITZGERALD
Tender is the Night
The Great Gatsby

GUSTAVE FLAUBERT
Madame Bovary

E. M. FORSTER
A Passage to India
Howards End

JOHN FOWLES
The French Lieutenant's Woman

ATHOL FUGARD
Selected Plays

JOHN GALSWORTHY
Strife

MRS GASKELL
North and South

WILLIAM GOLDING
Lord of the Flies
The Spire

OLIVER GOLDSMITH
She Stoops to Conquer
The Vicar of Wakefield

ROBERT GRAVES
Goodbye to All That

GRAHAM GREENE
Brighton Rock
The Heart of the Matter
The Power and the Glory

WILLIS HALL
The Long and the Short and the Tall

THOMAS HARDY
Far from the Madding Crowd
Jude the Obscure
Selected Poems
Tess of the D'Urbervilles
The Mayor of Casterbridge
The Return of the Native
The Trumpet Major
The Woodlanders
Under the Greenwood Tree

L. P. HARTLEY
The Go-Between
The Shrimp and the Anemone

NATHANIEL HAWTHORNE
The Scarlet Letter

SEAMUS HEANEY
Selected Poems

JOSEPH HELLER
Catch-22

ERNEST HEMINGWAY
A Farewell to Arms
For Whom the Bell Tolls
The Old Man and the Sea

GEORGE HERBERT
Selected Poems

HERMANN HESSE
Steppenwolf

BARRY HINES
Kes

HOMER
The Iliad
The Odyssey

ANTHONY HOPE
The Prisoner of Zenda

GERARD MANLEY HOPKINS
Selected Poems

WILLIAM DEAN HOWELLS
The Rise of Silas Lapham

RICHARD HUGHES
A High Wind in Jamaica

TED HUGHES
Selected Poems

THOMAS HUGHES
Tom Brown's Schooldays

ALDOUS HUXLEY
Brave New World

HENRIK IBSEN
A Doll's House
Ghosts

HENRY JAMES
Daisy Miller
The Ambassadors
The Europeans
The Portrait of a Lady
The Turn of the Screw
Washington Square

SAMUEL JOHNSON
Rasselas

BEN JONSON
The Alchemist
Volpone

JAMES JOYCE
A Portrait of the Artist as a Young Man
Dubliners

JOHN KEATS
Selected Poems

RUDYARD KIPLING
Kim

D. H. LAWRENCE
Sons and Lovers
The Rainbow
Women in Love

CAMARA LAYE
L'Enfant Noir

HARPER LEE
To Kill a Mocking-Bird

LAURIE LEE
Cider with Rosie

THOMAS MANN
Tonio Kröger

CHRISTOPHER MARLOWE
Doctor Faustus

ANDREW MARVELL
Selected Poems

W. SOMERSET MAUGHAM
Selected Short Stories

GAVIN MAXWELL
Ring of Bright Water

J. MEADE FALKNER
Moonfleet

HERMAN MELVILLE
Billy Budd
Moby Dick

THOMAS MIDDLETON
Women Beware Women

THOMAS MIDDLETON *and* WILLIAM ROWLEY
The Changeling

ARTHUR MILLER
A View from the Bridge
Death of a Salesman
The Crucible

JOHN MILTON
Paradise Lost I & II
Paradise Lost IV & IX
Selected Poems

V. S. NAIPAUL
A House for Mr Biswas

ROBERT O'BRIEN
Z for Zachariah

SEAN O'CASEY
Juno and the Paycock

GABRIEL OKARA
The Voice

EUGENE O'NEILL
Mourning Becomes Electra

GEORGE ORWELL
Animal Farm
Nineteen Eighty-four

JOHN OSBORNE
Look Back in Anger

WILFRED OWEN
Selected Poems

ALAN PATON
Cry, The Beloved Country

THOMAS LOVE PEACOCK
Nightmare Abbey and *Crotchet Castle*

HAROLD PINTER
The Caretaker

PLATO
The Republic

ALEXANDER POPE
Selected Poems

J. B. PRIESTLEY
An Inspector Calls

THOMAS PYNCHON
The Crying of Lot 49

SIR WALTER SCOTT
Ivanhoe
Quentin Durward
The Heart of Midlothian
Waverley

PETER SHAFFER
The Royal Hunt of the Sun

WILLIAM SHAKESPEARE
A Midsummer Night's Dream
Antony and Cleopatra
As You Like It
Coriolanus
Cymbeline
Hamlet
Henry IV Part I
Henry IV Part II
Henry V
Julius Caesar
King Lear
Love's Labour's Lost
Macbeth
Measure for Measure
Much Ado About Nothing
Othello
Richard II
Richard III
Romeo and Juliet
Sonnets
The Merchant of Venice
The Taming of the Shrew
The Tempest
The Winter's Tale
Troilus and Cressida
Twelfth Night

GEORGE BERNARD SHAW
Androcles and the Lion
Arms and the Man
Caesar and Cleopatra
Candida
Major Barbara
Pygmalion
Saint Joan
The Devil's Disciple

MARY SHELLEY
Frankenstein

PERCY BYSSHE SHELLEY
Selected Poems

RICHARD BRINSLEY SHERIDAN
The School for Scandal
The Rivals

R. C. SHERRIFF
Journey's End

WOLE SOYINKA
The Road
Three Short Plays

EDMUND SPENSER
The Faerie Queene (Book I)

JOHN STEINBECK
Of Mice and Men
The Grapes of Wrath
The Pearl

LAURENCE STERNE
A Sentimental Journey
Tristram Shandy

ROBERT LOUIS STEVENSON
Kidnapped
Treasure Island
Dr Jekyll and Mr Hyde

TOM STOPPARD
Professional Foul
Rosencrantz and Guildenstern are Dead

JONATHAN SWIFT
Gulliver's Travels

JOHN MILLINGTON SYNGE
The Playboy of the Western World

TENNYSON
Selected Poems

W. M. THACKERAY
Vanity Fair

DYLAN THOMAS
Under Milk Wood

EDWARD THOMAS
Selected Poems

FLORA THOMPSON
Lark Rise to Candleford

J. R. R. TOLKIEN
The Hobbit
The Lord of the Rings

ANTHONY TROLLOPE
Barchester Towers

MARK TWAIN
Huckleberry Finn
Tom Sawyer

JOHN VANBRUGH
The Relapse

VIRGIL
The Aeneid

VOLTAIRE
Candide

KEITH WATERHOUSE
Billy Liar

EVELYN WAUGH
Decline and Fall

JOHN WEBSTER
The Duchess of Malfi
The White Devil

H. G. WELLS
The History of Mr Polly
The Invisible Man
The War of the Worlds

OSCAR WILDE
The Importance of Being Earnest

THORNTON WILDER
Our Town

TENNESSEE WILLIAMS
The Glass Menagerie

VIRGINIA WOOLF
Mrs Dalloway
To the Lighthouse

WILLIAM WORDSWORTH
Selected Poems

WILLIAM WYCHERLEY
The Country Wife

W. B. YEATS
Selected Poems